WE

We hold these truths to be self-evident, that all men are created equal, that they are endowed by their Creator with certain unalienable Rights, that among these are Life, Liberty, and the pursuit of Happiness.

—U.S. DECLARATION OF INDEPENDENCE

We the People of the United States, in Order to form a more perfect Union, establish Justice, insure domestic Tranquility, provide for the common Defense, promote the general Welfare, and secure the Blessings of Liberty to ourselves and our Posterity, do ordain and establish this Constitution for the United States of America.

—U.S. CONSTITUTION

My fellow Americans, ask not what your country can do for you, ask what you can do for your country.

—JOHN F. KENNEDY, INAUGURAL ADDRESS

Do unto others as you would have them do unto you.

—THE GOLDEN RULE (VARIOUS VERSIONS)
BAHA'I, BUDDHISM, CHRISTIANITY, CONFUCIANISM, ISLAM,
JUDAISM, NATIVE AMERICAN SPIRITUALITY, AND OTHERS

A house divided against itself cannot stand.

—ABRAHAM LINCOLN

Reprinted with permission

WE THE PEOPLE

WE THE PEOPLE

RESTORING CIVILITY,
SANITY, *and*
UNIFYING SOLUTIONS
to U.S. POLITICS

H. EDWARD WYNN

HOUNDSTOOTH PRESS

WE THE PEOPLE

Restoring Civility, Sanity, and Unifying Solutions to U.S. Politics

ISBN   978-1-5445-1495-6 *Hardcover*
        978-1-5445-1494-9 *Paperback*
        978-1-5445-1493-2 *Ebook*

This book is dedicated to all those who have had and have the courage, despite personal attacks and bitter betrayals, to work tirelessly to find common ground in the midst of partisan loyalties and unifying solutions in the face of divisiveness and extremism.

CONTENTS

PART III: REFRAMING OUR DISCOURSE

PART IV: EXAMPLES AND POTENTIAL SOLUTIONS

FOR(E)WARD

(FOREWORD TO THIS BOOK AND FORWARD—HOPEFULLY—TO BETTER POLITICAL DISCOURSE AND SOLUTIONS)

"It was the best of times; it was the worst of times" is the beginning of one of my favorite books, Charles Dickens's *A Tale of Two Cities*. Written about events more than two centuries ago, that sentence could have been written about virtually any time in history. We all tend to believe that the time in which we live is paradoxically both the best and worst of times. Correspondingly, we tend to view our yesterday as better than it objectively was, and our tomorrow as either providing significantly more or less promise than today, depending on our level of optimism or pessimism.

Our perception of the present time, call it the information technology age, is not any different. On the one hand, we view it as the "best of times," the access to information and technology we have has been unlike that of any other generation. We have all become so dependent on smartphones, social media, and the internet that we can hardly imagine how the world existed without these things. Yet, we bemoan what we perceive as the "worst" of the current time, including violence, both physical and verbal, and a lack of civility among us. If this were written a half century ago, two centuries ago like *Tale of Two Cities*, or would be written a half century or two centuries from now, we would find similar "bests" and "worsts."

Debating whether today is either the best or the worst compared to other time periods is pointless and destructive. It is pointless because there is not a competition to be the "best" or "worst," nor are such superlatives meaningful. Each generation, each period of time, has had—and will have—its "bests" and "worsts."

It is destructive because it distracts us from focusing on what we should be focusing on—how to make our time both better and—pardon the grammar—less worse.

There are a lot of political, sociological, anthropological, and philosophical writings that, quite frankly, pander to the emotions that this pointless debate elicits, including, but by no means limited to, Margolis and Noonan's *The Worst President in History: The Legacy of Barack Obama* and on the other side, Wilson's *Everything Trump Touches Dies: A Republican Strategist Gets Real About the Worst President Ever.* And how I wish that the title of Michiko Kakutani's *The Death of Truth: Notes on Falsehood in the Age of Trump* would have stopped before the colon and would have taken a more bipartisan approach, since that book contains many, many excellent points. These titles and content may sell books or generate clicks or screen views, but these words tend—knowingly or not—to worsen the woes they exclaim rather than making them better.

How do they do this? Rather than rallying us together to help us better our bests and lessen our worsts, they divide and polarize us. What is particularly disappointing is that many of these writings have some kernels of truth and even wisdom that we should all consider as we seek to improve, to heal, to unite, and to be civil with each other.

This is particularly true of the many significant policy debates in our country today, including immigration, gun violence, and climate policy.

What follows are thoughts, with facts to support those thoughts, based on a fervent and urgent desire to cause us to come together: (1) to add to that discussion facts, real facts, without emotional charge, (2) to consider all fact-based viewpoints, especially those that are different from our own, (3) to work from a sense of common purpose and commitment to agree on what we can do and then do it with courage and commitment to each other, and (4) civilly and with caring to agree to disagree on the rest, keeping open a dialogue when new facts and information arise, or a new perspective arises based on those facts and information.

To do this—based on decades of experience in solving complex issues in highly divisive and polarizing contexts, including specific experience with federal, state, and local governments in all three governmental branches and in Republican and Democratic administrations—I believe that we need to do three things:

- Define our mutual purpose.
- Gather relevant facts and information.
- Consider alternate solutions and select those solutions that best align with our mutual purpose and those facts and that information.

As simple as this may sound, it is by no means easy. And once those solutions are identified, they will need to be implemented—also not easy.

But before we can even begin that journey, we need to focus on what the vast majority of us would clearly agree on: the lack of civility in public discourse. Perhaps it is worse now than ever, or perhaps it only appears that way given today's vastly greater amount of and access to information. But as noted above, whether it is the worst or not is irrelevant. What is relevant is that it exists, as well as understanding why it exists, how it is harmful, and most important of all, how to change it.

The power to change this lack of civility among us lies not with politicians or business leaders, the media, or spiritual or religious leaders. The power to change this lack of civility lies with us and us alone. Although politicians, the media, and others may have participated in this lack of civility—and perhaps even given it greater voice and power—we willingly participated in it. Without our participation, it will no longer have a voice or power.

Let's put aside blame, defeatism, prejudice, whatever holds us back from creating civility among us so that we can productively discuss—and resolve—the significant issues that we face.

We each have the power to take simple actions individually and collectively to determine how we can better interact and communicate with each other. And in doing so, we can solve many of the significant issues that face us, just as we have throughout history. Because then and now:

- We solve more issues in a discussion than in an argument.
- There is more that unites us than divides us.

- We are much better, individually and collectively, when we are united rather than divided.
- We have the power to change whatever divides us.
- We have the power to make our bests even better and to lessen our worsts.
- Working together, we have the power: the power of We the People.

INTRODUCTION

SO WHAT?

Before we begin our journey, let's start with why we, and you, should go on this journey. Why should we, should you, care about civics or about political discourse?

Increasingly, many of us believe and, I would posit, are being pushed toward believing by those in power that there is no good reason to care about politics. Both parties, and especially those at the extremes in either party, want us to believe that politics is complicated and dirty. They don't want us to recognize what's really going on, what the facts are, or how to spot the lies and deception. That is why we get spin, emotional appeals, and conspiracy theories instead of facts, and it's also why those who attempt to return us to the facts and help spot the lies and deception are met with verbal (sometimes even physical) violence and intimidation.

Getting the facts is also hard—and it's getting even harder. Few have time to read the source documents or to otherwise discover the facts themselves, and we can no longer trust a polarized and point-of-view media to summarize those facts in an unbiased manner. As social media has driven us to information-by-tweet, this problem has become even worse.

We might also believe that it doesn't matter: even if we were able to get the facts and spot the lies and deception, it wouldn't change anything. That is really unfortunate because it demonstrates that we have been indoctrinated to believe that we are powerless over governments that are supposed to derive their power from us.

It's a lot like school bullying. Most such bullying starts with just a few people who are loud and appear to be powerful. They intimidate the majority to go along with their behavior to avoid any issues. When someone does stand up, they are immediately intimidated or harassed as a warning to others so that the bullies maintain their control. In reality, the majority doesn't really agree with what the bullies are doing, but they feel powerless to stop it.

The point is this: We the People can—and must—make a difference. The overwhelming majority of us agree that we do not like the current way politics are conducted in the United States. We don't like the divisiveness, the verbal and physical violence, the lack of solutions. If we, the overwhelming majority, don't like the current state, why do we continue to accept it?

We don't have to.

Because we are the overwhelming majority, we have the power to make a difference and no longer need to be intimidated by the extremes, by those in power, or by the divisiveness and violence. Working together, we can change all of this.

Yes, it will require each of us to educate ourselves about things that we should have been taught about civics but weren't. It will require each of us to spot the causes of lack of civility in political discourse when they arise and to use simple solutions to turn that lack of civility and that divisiveness into unifying solutions. We can reject biased, point-of-view media by something as simple as just turning off those outlets and turning to more fact-based sources of information.

For sure, changing the current state will take time, just like any significant change. That change will be met by formidable resistance from those who seek to preserve the power they derive from the current state. But We the People have the power, the legal and constitutional power and, perhaps most importantly, the power of being the majority.

Just imagine for a moment what this change would look and feel like:

- Political ads that focus on policies, not personal attacks on opponents.
- Resolving the most important issues we face together by focusing on the facts and having civil debate and discussion of our mutual objectives and potential solutions.
- Feeling that we can discuss those important issues and solutions with our colleagues, neighbors, even our families without shouting or changing the topic, or getting that generally sick feeling in our stomachs, or getting emotionally out of control.
- Reconnecting our communities and feeling a renewed sense of purpose, security, and safety.

Sounds great, doesn't it?

We can achieve it. It is within your power, my power, and our power. The power of We the People.

PART I

UNDERSTANDING THE U.S. POLITICAL PROCESS: WHAT YOU NEED TO KNOW THAT YOU WEREN'T TAUGHT IN CIVICS

INTRODUCTION AND OVERVIEW

> ### TL; DR
>
> *Note: Even though each chapter and section is relatively succinct, for those who wish to have an even more succinct summary, I'll begin each chapter or significant section of this part with a box labeled with the internet/social media acronym "TL; DR" (Too Long; Didn't Read), summarizing the most important points in that chapter or section. Hopefully, you'll read on, but the choice is yours.*
>
> - Civics education hasn't taught us what we need to know to participate in and influence our governments.
> - Despite increased information, we lack relevant and trustworthy information and how to assess information for relevance and truth.

In most, if not all, U.S. states, students are required to pass a civics test in order to graduate from junior or senior high school. In preparing for that test, students are taught a litany of statistics about government. In today's information age, most of this information can easily be Googled and obtained virtually instantaneously. Knowing that there are 435 congressional representatives and one hundred U.S. senators, however, imparts very little knowledge about how government works in the United States and even less about how we can be active and responsible citizens. Civics, as taught in U.S. schools today, tends to focus more on these statistics and similar data rather than on the "so whats?"—that is, what do these statistics and data tell us about our government and how we can be active and responsible citizens. For example, ask one hundred people on the street (of any age group) why there are 435 congressional representatives and U.S. senators and what this means in terms of significant aspects of the federal political process, and few of those could give an answer that would merit a passing grade.

This is the failure, and has been the failure, of civics education in the United States, not only now but throughout several generations.

The result, as demonstrated by study after study, is a relative ignorance of the political process in the United States, federal, state, or local.[1]

Asked today why they don't vote, many millennials say they don't have sufficient knowledge to be able to make a decision.[2] This is absolutely remarkable in today's information age, when such knowledge should be available at the touch of a screen or the stroke of a keyboard.

As a result, we are left vulnerable to misinformation, unable to sort out the facts from the misrepresentations, to sort out the relevant from the irrelevant, and to understand why our political system has stopped working for us.

Unfortunately, providing the basic critical information and reasoning skills needed for each of us to participate more fully and actively as citizens has only become more difficult. It is politically and socially safe to teach just the statistics and data; discussing the "so-whats" subjects the informer to attack because those "so-whats" may not align with an individual's or group's partisan beliefs.[3]

This must change, and that change must start with us.

In the immediately following chapters, you'll learn the most important things about how each level of our government works—

things you almost certainly did not learn in a civics class. We will do this from the perspective of how each of us can understand why each level of government operates as it does, why that is important, and how it shapes political debate and decision-making, as well as how each of us can have a greater role in shaping that debate and decision-making.

This exploration cannot possibly cover every detail of each level of government. For state governments, it cannot comprehensively identify individual state differences. Instead, it is intended to provide the information and concepts most relevant to our understanding and participating most effectively at every level of government.

CHAPTER I

THE MOST IMPORTANT THINGS YOU NEED TO KNOW ABOUT PRESIDENTIAL ELECTIONS

TL; DR

- Presidents have term limits so they don't accumulate too much power.
- As a practical matter, a presidential candidate must obtain the nomination of his or her political party to become president.
- Money and influence are currently the two most important factors in determining presidential candidates, but we can change this.
- Political Action Committees (PACs), super PACs, and bundlers have significant influence in presidential party nominations and elections. Super PACs have the greatest influence.
- The real audience in presidential party candidate debates are bundlers and influencers, not us.
- We may not have the final say as to which candidate each political party nominates for the presidency.

- Some states, especially smaller ones, have greater influence in determining each party's presidential nominee.
- U.S. presidents are not and have never been elected based on the total vote of all U.S. voters, often called the popular vote. They are elected based on electoral votes.
- About 75 percent of the electoral votes are locked in before the election process even begins!
- In determining electoral votes, votes in some states matter more than votes in other states.
- Be skeptical of presidential polling results; they may not be a representative sample of actual voters.
- After they are elected, presidents reward big donors and supporters with government jobs and business, regardless of qualifications. This is known as patronage.

PRESIDENTIAL TERM LIMITS

Why is the president limited to two four-year terms? The original Constitution did not provide a limit on the president's term. That came about as a result of the Twenty-Second Amendment to the Constitution, after the death of President Franklin D. Roosevelt, who was the nation's longest serving president. (Just prior to his death, he was elected to a fourth term in office.) The rationale behind that amendment was to limit the accumulation of presidential power as a result of a president being in office a long period of time. For example, a president who served unlimited terms could "pack" the Supreme Court with justices aligned with his or her[4] ideologies, decreasing the likelihood that Supreme Court judges would rule unfavorably to the president during his or her term of office. Even after that term, because Supreme Court justices are appointed for life, a long-serving president could influence the court for multiple generations.

If a president is elected to a second four-year term, that president is called a lame duck. This means that since the president does not have to worry about being reelected again—he or she can't be—he or she will presumably make decisions that are the right thing to do, even if not popular. However, a "lame duck" president could also make decisions that are in his or her own best interest or to help favored individuals and companies, even if those decisions are not popular. Presumably, though, the next president could undo many or most of those decisions.

PRESIDENTIAL ELECTIONS

The most important part of this process is not even in the Constitution: as a practical matter, a presidential candidate must receive the nomination of a political party to be elected president. Indeed, the United States has NEVER elected a president who did not receive the nomination of his political party. Why is this so important? In order to receive the nomination of his or her political party, a presidential candidate must obtain the approval of members of that party through its given political structure. This has a very significant effect on whom we choose as president. And selecting the presidential nominee is much, much more complicated than each of us voting in a primary and whoever wins the primary is the nominee. It doesn't even work that way.

In a nutshell—and this is true for understanding many, many other aspects of our political process in the United States—that party nomination process is primarily about two things: money and influence.

This is not a politically jaundiced, politically cynical comment. It is also not a statement of defeatism. Just because money and influence may be important doesn't mean that we, as common citizens who may not be mega-millionaire political donors and/ or highly connected individuals, cannot have an impact on the political process. Indeed, the information age provides us with great potential to have a substantial role in the political process. But, like with many things, we have to understand how the process works to be able to influence it or change it.

It is also not a partisan statement. Money and influence are nonpartisan. They determine Republican nominees just as they determine Democratic nominees. Please avoid the temptation to assign money and influence as belonging solely to one party: the facts don't support that, not at all.

Nor does this mean that money and influence are the only factors that determine who leaders are, or that only the superrich and superpowerful can have money and influence, nor that the superrich or superpowerful are "villains." The issue is the process, not the people who are part of that process.

THE NOMINATION PROCESS

First, someone has to identify themselves as a potential candidate. Ever wonder why most candidates, particularly those without national name recognition, start out by forming an "exploratory committee" or something similar? That's to "test the waters" to see if that candidate has the ability to gain enough support from key donors and political influencers to make that individual's campaign viable. These "exploratory committees" are principally about…money and influence. There's no voting by us to determine whether we want this person as a candidate. Potential candidates may do opinion polls, but those polls are not an election and are far from unbiased. Their purpose is to promote the candidacy of the potential candidate to those donors and influencers.

For sure, there may be other reasons that a potential candidate may "announce" their candidacy, including signaling to opponents to not become candidates, but generally, exploratory committees are all about fishing for money and influencers.

This is because running for any office, but especially for president of the United States, is very expensive. The total campaign costs of both candidates in the 2016 presidential election was $6.8 *billion*.[5] The United States doesn't really have publicly funded federal (or state) campaigns. Although funds are collected for such funding, the funding is rarely used because to receive those funds, a candidate must limit private campaign contributions to the amount of the public funds they could receive.[6] In 2016, that amount was a paltry $96 million.[7]

How do candidates get financial support?

One way is from "bundlers." Bundlers are very well-connected individuals or families who have a strong track record of being able to raise large amounts of money from others.[8] Of course, bundlers want to make sure that the potential candidate's positions align with theirs and those from whom they solicit contributions. As a result, bundlers have—and have had—influence on candidates' positions before the election, on getting people appointed to key positions in the successful candidate's administration and even obtaining government business or contracts.

There are other sources, too, especially political action committees (PACs) and super PACs, and even other current officeholders, who can donate money from their campaign funds to other candidates.

What are PACs and super PACs and why are they so important?

Regular PACs are highly regulated. Contributions are limited, both in amount and source. No direct corporate, union, or other group contributions are permitted. PACs are the way that those groups can "contribute" *indirectly* to political candidates by leveraging contributions from individuals who are part of these groups. Since the PAC's influence depends on the amount and number of individual contributors to the PAC, these companies or groups often pressure their executives, employees, or members of the group to contribute to the PAC. Those contributions are often personally solicited by group leaders (e.g., your boss or your boss's boss, or a union steward or union leader) and contributions may be made through payroll deductions. Thus, PACs can generate political contributions that employees generally would not make or might make to candidates other than those the PAC supports.

Super PACs can't make direct contributions to a candidate or coordinate with a candidate's campaign, but they can do so much more! Unlike PACs, super PACS can raise money from anyone, including corporations and unions, without any contribution limitations! Instead of making direct candidate contributions, super PACs spend the money they raise to advocate for a particular candidate or cause. They adopt innocuous or euphemistic names that make it difficult to understand who is really behind the super PAC.[9] Because of all of this, but especially because of the unlimited source and amount of contributions, super PACs can have substantial influence on primary and general elections by financing multimillion-dollar advertising campaigns in support of candidates.

Even though some partisan groups decry the Supreme Court's decision (*Citizens United*), which established the legality of super PACs, those same partisan groups have formed, funded, and extensively used super PACs themselves in federal (and state) elections.

PRESIDENTIAL DEBATES

How do presidential debates play into this? Debates are a way to winnow a large pool of candidates for a particular political party. For example, in the 2016 election there were at least seventeen Republican candidates; there were more than twenty Democratic candidates for the 2020 election. Each political party has established financial and polling thresholds to directly exclude candidates with little public and financial support. As a result, bundlers and influencers (including super PACs) have a substantial role in winnowing the pool of candidates. To continue to get money from these individuals and groups, candidates have to show that they can win by obtaining favorable poll results and other donations. Without that support, they won't meet the party-established financial and polling thresholds that enable them to make it to the next debate round.

To bolster their own standing and/or to diminish competing candidates' standing, a candidate tries to find an opponent's weakness and exploit it (even if such an attack lacks facts), so-called "gotcha" politics. The goal? Create a "breakout" moment—even (and especially) if it embarrasses a fellow candidate. That's why direct candidate attacks (e.g., Senator Elizabeth Warren's takedown of Mike Bloomberg in one of the Democratic candidate debates in the 2020 presidential election) can be so powerful.

A candidate also tries to demonstrate that his or her viewpoints are more aligned with those of party influencers. This is why moderators ask candidates to agree with identified positions associated with that political party (e.g., asking 2020 Democratic presidential candidates whether illegal immigrants should have government-provided healthcare). Not associating yourself with that position is risky: such a candidate must either have to have a good reason for not doing so—for example, taking an even more polarized position or concisely and convincingly explaining a flaw in the statement of the position.

Who decides if a candidate did well in a debate? There may be voter polling at some point, which in itself may be biased or focused on a handful of early voting/caucusing states. But the most immediate "decision makers" are the news media analysts who tell everyone who "won" or "lost."

As with many things, money talks. That's why Kamala Harris in her closing remarks at the first 2020 Democratic presidential debate pitched donating to her campaign and gave her website address. It apparently worked (along with her debate performance). She raised $2 million in just twenty-four hours after the first Democratic candidate debate.[10] Conversely, later, lack of money is why Senator Harris was forced to end her campaign.

To further demonstrate this point, if a candidate stumbles in a debate, they don't launch ads or social media posts or mainstream media appearances to the general public to regain their footing. They go to certain political influencers to help change negative reaction of certain voting groups to the stumble and to get that influencer/those influencers to "cleanse" the stumbling candidate.[11] For example, candidate Joe Biden met with Jesse Jackson Sr., of the Rainbow PUSH Coalition, a national civil rights organization, after fellow candidate Kamala Harris attacked Biden's civil rights record. Biden obtained a statement from Mr. Jackson that he was persuaded that Biden had changed his position from those Senator Harris had attacked.

PRIMARIES AND CAUCUSES

What are primaries and caucuses? Why are small states so influential in the presidential nomination process?

In short, it's all about being first. States (and state political parties) want to have strong influence (there we go again with the influence) on the selection of the presidential nominee (or their party's nominee). How do they do this? They have their primary or caucus first or very early. For example, Iowa has just six (out of the 538 total) electoral votes, but winning the first-in-the-nation Iowa caucus usually gives "front-runner" advantage to a winning candidate. Being that front-runner attracts more—you guessed it—money and influencers. That's why smaller states can have such a big influence in presidential elections.[12]

Although being first or early is important, so is being the "right" state. A "right" state is a so-called battleground or litmus-test state. A battleground state is one that will likely determine the outcome of the election. A litmus-test state is one that generally has been successful at selecting the winning presidential candidate. This is why both who wins primaries in these states and the specific voter groups they win in these states are so important. For example, Presidential Candidate Joe Biden's 2020 primary win in Michigan, a battleground state, was significant because he won convincingly in counties and with voter groups that his primary opponent, Bernie Sanders, won in the 2016 primary and which Donald Trump won in the 2016 general election.

Therefore, it is important to understand how each party selects its presidential candidate in caucuses and primaries.

A caucus is a method of choosing a party's presidential candidate, run by that party and consisting only of registered party members who show up at the place and time of the caucus. At the caucus, party members separate into groups based on the candidate they support, and then advocates for other candidates try to get attendees to change their vote. Thus, caucus results will not reflect the view of independent voters (only registered party members may attend) and may not reflect the view of all or most party members. This is for several reasons. First, a candidate can pack a caucus with his or her supporters and then use those supporters to overwhelm any undecided caucus members or those who support minority candidates. Among other factors, caucus participants may be friends or neighbors, so unlike in a secret ballot primary, peer or other pressures may influence the results. Even when and where a caucus is held may influence the results—a weekday evening caucus may exclude non-day-shift workers, single parents, and other demographics. Because most caucuses are held early in the election cycle, lesser known candidates can focus their more limited organizations and resources on caucus states to attempt to gain front-runner status and thereby, more money and influencers for later primaries.

Ten states (and three territories) choose candidates of one or both parties using a caucus.

A primary is an election where registered voters get to decide a party's candidate for president (and other offices). In a primary, you have to choose one party's ballot and only vote for that party's candidates. Primaries are either closed, semi-closed, or open. Closed means that you can only vote in the primary if you are registered as a party member (no independent voters may vote), and you can only vote for the candidates of the party for which you registered. In a semi-closed primary, independent voters can choose which party to vote for, but registered voters can only vote for the candidates of the party with which they are registered. In an open primary, you can choose which party's ballot you will take regardless of whether you are a member of that party or any party.

Democratic primaries in fourteen states are closed, eleven are semi-closed, and the rest are open. Republican primaries are closed in twenty-one states, semi-closed in seven, and the rest are open.

What does this mean?

- In a closed primary (a little more than 25 percent of Democratic primaries and a little more than 40 percent of Republican primaries), if you are an independent (unaffiliated with a party), you are prohibited from choosing a presidential candidate in that state. (The same is true for a caucus state since only registered party members may participate in a caucus.)
- In open primary states, it is possible—and there is some evidence that this has happened—for one party with a dominant candidate to have its party's supporters vote in the *other party's* primary with the intent of choosing the candidate of the other party who is viewed as the easier opponent in the general election or to prolong a fight between one party's presidential candidates.[13]

The goal: win in the first and early primaries and caucuses, and win the most populous states dominated by your party. Why is this the case? To win a party's nomination, you have to win the largest number of party delegates. The number of delegates in each state is based on the population of the state and the number of that party's voters there. Thus, the largest number of delegates is often, but not always, in the states with the largest electoral votes. For example, a Democratic candidate would certainly want to win California and New York (predominately Democratic states with large populations and the greatest number of Democratic delegates). Conversely, winning in a low-population state that is dominated by the other party will get you many, many fewer delegates.

This raises the issue of superdelegates, which are not selected based on primary or caucus results but are elite party members (e.g., current elected officials, former presidents and vice presidents, and other party leaders). The idea behind this was that party leaders knew best about which candidates were electable, even if voters and caucus goers thought otherwise. (Sounds a little elitist—and maybe just a touch arrogant—right?) About 15 percent of Democratic and 7 percent of Republican delegates are superdelegates.

Why does this matter?

In the 2016 Democratic primary process, Presidential Candidate Bernie Sanders raised concerns that Presidential Candidate Hillary Clinton had overwhelming support from superdelegates and that she could use that support to win the nomination, even if Sanders had more regular delegates. As a result, the Democratic Party limited the role of superdelegates in 2016, and in 2018, further reformed their role, providing that superdelegates cannot vote in the first round of balloting for a Democratic presidential nominee.[14]

THE ELECTORAL COLLEGE: THE VOTES THAT REALLY MATTER

First of all, there's no real "college." The Electoral College refers to people and a process. The people: delegates chosen by each state to cast a vote for president and vice president after each presidential election. The number of delegates in each state is the total number of congressional representatives in that state plus two (the number of senators in each state).[15] Each of these delegates pledges to vote for the candidate that won their state's presidential election. It's winner takes all except in two states. More on that later.

Let's be clear:

- Technically and actually, U.S. presidents are not and have never been elected based on the total vote of all U.S. voters, called the popular vote.
- To win the presidency, the president must obtain the majority vote of the Electoral College. (Since there are a total of 538 electoral votes [435 congressional representatives, one hundred senators, and three electoral votes of the District of Columbia], a candidate must receive half plus one of those votes—that is, 270 electoral votes.)

The Electoral College is about weighting. On the one hand, the most populous states have the most electoral votes—for example, California, our most populous state, has fifty-five electoral votes, and seven states, because they each have only one congressional representative, each have just three votes. As a result of giving every state three electoral votes regardless of their population, smaller states have a slight proportional advantage in the number of electoral votes than they would have if the number of electoral votes were based only on population.

Why was this done? The thought was that highly populous states shouldn't be allowed to overwhelm the voters in less populous states. (This is also the reason there are two senators from each state.) Good or bad, it's designed to give a little more weight to less populous states than they would have on a purely per capita (per person) basis.

However, the biggest potential weighting effect of the Electoral

College is the fact that in every state except Maine (three electoral votes) and Nebraska (five electoral votes),[16] it's winner takes all—that is, if you have 50 percent plus one vote in that state, you get ALL of that state's electoral votes—the same number of electoral votes as if you won *every* person's vote in that state. This is exactly why a candidate can win the electoral vote, and therefore the presidency, even if he or she doesn't win the popular vote. *Indeed, a president could win as little as 23 percent of the popular vote and still win the electoral vote.*[17]

That, in 2016, it was so surprising to so many of us that a candidate could win the election and lose the popular vote demonstrates that current civics education is not sufficient. Indeed, this was neither the first nor only election where this occurred.[18] Here's the other kicker to this: *even before the election takes place,* about 75 percent of electoral votes, in states that are overwhelmingly Democratic or Republican, are locked in. Each party's nominee won't fight (or sometimes even campaign) in these states, since getting one extra vote or a hundred, or a thousand, or a million extra votes in those states doesn't matter. The candidate of the dominant party in that state is certain to get at least 50 percent plus one vote in that state. If you live in such a state—as I currently do—it is almost guaranteed that your state's electoral votes will go to that predominate party's candidate, since it is virtually impossible for the nondominant party candidate to receive more than 50 percent of that state's vote. California's, New York's, and Illinois's electoral votes have gone to the Democratic candidate in every election after 1988; Arizona's electoral votes have gone to the Republican candidate in every presidential election since 1960, except for 1996—when President Bill Clinton won the Electoral College in a landslide.

Indeed, more than a year before the 2020 presidential election,

270towin.com already determined—before the first party debates and even before we knew all the candidates who were running—that in the 2020 presidential election, 183 electoral votes are safe Democratic, and 125 electoral votes are safe Republican, with an additional twenty-seven and fifty-six electoral votes as likely for each respective party's candidate, leaving only 147 electoral votes (about 27 percent of the total) in eleven states with a reasonable chance to be at all decisional. Just five of those states (Arizona, Wisconsin, Michigan, Pennsylvania, and Florida) were in the "toss-up" category. These states are called the battleground states.[19]

This is why, during the general election campaign, you'll see ads and campaign events in those states and not in the "locked-in" states. In the battleground states, your vote counts A LOT and, in fact, can determine the outcome of the election. Why? If your vote is that plus one (over 50 percent), all the electoral votes for that state go to the candidate that got your vote. If you're the Democratic candidate, getting a hundred thousand extra votes in California won't get you any closer to the presidency. But getting that extra vote in Florida, a battleground state, may win the election.

POLLING

First, think about how pollsters contact voters when conducting a poll. There is a predominant reliance on "home" (i.e., landline) telephone numbers. These have been the staple of pollsters since virtually everyone had a landline phone and their phone number identified the geography of the owner. This has changed with the increasing use of cellular phones and the demise of landline phones. Cellular phone numbers may not be as readily available to pollsters and do not necessarily identify the owner's current voting state or district since we tend to keep our cell phone number when we relocate. Polling that relies too heavily on landline phone numbers can affect the results. It will tend to exclude those who do not have a landline phone, and to the extent the demographic of remaining landline phone owners is different than the general populace, the results from such polling may be skewed. Before drawing conclusions from any poll, read (often in fine print) the details on how the poll was conducted to see if the sample is flawed because of this change in technology.

Second, only people who actually vote matter for polling. However, many people are polled and their opinion recorded even though they will not vote in the actual election. Only about 50 percent of eligible voters actually vote. This can skew the results and can skew them even more if certain demographics have greater or lesser voter turnout and polling doesn't account for that. Some pollsters will ask if you will vote in the election, but some people may not admit to the pollster that they won't vote.

Third, as our elections and politics are more polarized, people may disguise their true voting preference because of perceived negative reactions to that choice. For example, in 2016, some polled voters were not willing to admit that they would vote for one of the certain presidential candidates because of a perceived negative reaction.

However, even if some polling results are flawed, don't let that keep you from voting. If the polls are right, maybe you had an influence on another federal, state, or local election. And if the polls are wrong, your vote may make a huge difference in determining who is our president. Remember, only about half of registered voters actually vote in an election. That's a lot of votes that can make a BIG difference in the outcome!

PATRONAGE

Once a particular candidate wins, he or she is going to give preference to those influencers and donors who helped him or her win. Not necessarily illegal, just a fact of life and human nature. Indeed, once a candidate wins (and sometimes even before), those influencers and donors are already lobbying for certain appointments (and in some cases, government business).

The best, most recent proof of this is the transcript of the testimony of former Secretary of State Rex Tillerson.[20] Former Secretary Tillerson describes the process for filling not only cabinet-level positions but also those reporting to those individuals and other positions subject to presidential appointment. It is evident that these positions are not filled based on qualifications but on political loyalties and that this screening left many critical positions unfilled for a long time in the Trump Administration.[21] By the way, this is the most recent example; this is equally true for Democratic presidents.[22]

Even though we expect a president to appoint individuals who are aligned with his or her goals and political positions, I don't think it's unreasonable to expect that the president appoint people who are also qualified. At the very least, such appointments should not be "pay to play"—that is, based on monetary contributions, especially from bundlers. Unfortunately, pay-to-play appointments happen, as most recently and publicly demonstrated by former Illinois Governor Rod Blagojevich, who, after he was caught trying to sell an appointment to the U.S. Senate seat vacated by President Obama, unsuccessfully argued that "this is just part of the political process."[23] Don't We the People find this completely offensive? If that's the process, it's time to change it.

CHAPTER 2

THE MOST IMPORTANT THINGS YOU NEED TO KNOW ABOUT THE FEDERAL GOVERNMENT

We were all taught the basics: the U.S. federal government has three branches: executive, legislative, and judicial. The legislative branch makes the laws, the executive branch carries out and enforces the laws, and the judicial branch interprets the laws. But that is a dramatic oversimplification of how the federal government works. The executive branch can, in fact, make laws; the legislative branch can, in fact, enforce certain laws; and the judiciary does make law in that in interpreting laws that Congress has passed or the president or administration has established, it creates its own body of law, known as case law.

Is such a tidy demarcation of responsibilities even helpful to us as citizens? Not really. To be helpful, we need to understand not only what the Constitution says about each branch of government, the letter of the law, so to speak, but also how it works and has worked.

We'll take each of the three federal government branches in turn and identify the most important things you need to know about that branch.

PRESIDENTIAL POWERS

TL; DR

- The president has substantial constitutional powers, including the power to veto legislation, a power that is rarely overridden.
- However, the president's most potent powers are not in the Constitution.

VETO POWER

The president's power to veto legislation that Congress passes is substantial. If he or she vetoes congressionally passed legislation, that legislation is dead unless two-thirds of *both* (this is key) houses of Congress vote to overturn the veto. Veto overrides are rare: fewer than 5 percent of presidential vetoes have been overridden.[24] One might assume that the only time that a presidential veto would be overturned is when the opposite party controls both chambers of Congress by a two-thirds or greater majority. However, presidential vetoes have been overridden even when the opposing party did not have a supermajority. Conversely, on the one occasion—so far—when a president faced an opposing party supermajority in both chambers of Congress—during President Andrew Johnson's presidency—almost half (48 percent) of his vetoes were not overturned.[25] Notably, no presidential veto has been overridden when the president has had a favorable supermajority in both congressional chambers.[26] This demonstrates that the veto power is a substantial one—one that can be used to block legislation that the president does not support, even though a majority of Congress does.

One of the most important presidential powers is not even mentioned in the Constitution: the power of the executive order.

An executive order is a way for a president to establish a policy or create a "law" without congressional approval.[27] Some of the most significant executive orders include the Emancipation Proclamation (freeing Southern slaves); the Japanese American Internment Order; orders establishing the Peace Corps, the Federal Emergency Management Agency, and the Office of Homeland Security; and orders ending the Trans-Pacific Trade Partnership and imposing a travel ban on residents of certain Middle East countries.

Executive orders can be challenged, and many have, but more often than not, they're upheld by the courts. Even if they're not upheld, they've been allowed to be in effect for a year or more while a challenge of the order makes its way through the courts.

The downside of executive orders? They can be undone by the next president, especially those of a former president of the opposing party. President Donald Trump issued fourteen such executive orders in his first week as president; President Barack Obama issued twelve in his first week as president.[28]

Another big power of the president is over foreign policy. Although we were taught in civics that the Senate has to approve treaties and that only Congress can declare war, in practice, neither of those congressional checks have stopped the president from doing much regarding foreign policy. Presidents have begun—without congressional approval or sometimes even without their advance knowledge—conflicts with other countries that are hard to distinguish from "war." (Examples include Iraq and Afghanistan, Korea and Vietnam.) Although Congress retains appropriation authority to fund a war, as a practical matter, Congress has never effectively used this power because of the perceived political repercussions of doing so. As we've also recently seen, although the Senate must *approve* treaties, the president can *un-approve* them. (Examples include President Trump's renunciation of the Climate Change and Iran treaties.)

What is the basis for the president's executive order and foreign policy power? If you saw the recent movie *Vice*, you know the answer: the unitary executive theory. That theory, based on the constitutional language giving the president all powers related to the executive branch, is that the president can direct the executive branch however he or she chooses, with very little restriction from Congress. Although presidential power under this theory significantly expanded during the administration of President George W. Bush and Vice President Dick Cheney, largely as a result of the 9/11 terrorist attacks, most modern presidents (both before and after) have also espoused it.[29]

The theory has some basis but up to a point. The president does have the power to direct the executive branch, including all executive agencies and employees without interference from Congress or the courts. This includes announcing when he or she will not enforce legislation enacted by Congress.[30] However, that power is not unlimited. It is subject to judicial review, upon appeal from an affected person or entity that finds such presidential direction unconstitutional or otherwise unlawful; and it is subject to Congress's powers of impeachment or constitutional amendment. But both of those are extraordinary remedies, rarely exercised successfully or at all. An easier and more recent frequently used check on presidential executive power is Congress's power to investigate the president and the executive branch.[31] More on that later.

Perhaps the most important power of the president is the power of influence. The president can attract media coverage more than any other individual on the planet and use that coverage to frame the debate on significant public policy issues. The president also has an almost unequaled ability to attract money for his or her campaign and for candidates of his or her party. The president's influence extends not only in the United States but also globally. To not recognize this constitutionally unstated power is to miss a significant presidential power.

There are certainly checks on presidential power by the other branches, whose checks are either more or less effective based on whether one or both houses of Congress have majorities of the same political party and the size of those majorities.[32] More about that in the upcoming section on Congress.

There is one presidential power that may be overrated: the power to appoint Supreme Court nominees. For sure, depending on the number of vacancies created during a president's term(s), he or she can appoint justices more closely aligned with his or her political philosophies, goals, and leanings. When the court acts with a closely divided majority (called 5–4 decisions, since there are nine Supreme Court justices, making five a majority), that power can correctly be perceived as potent. However, as history has shown (both longer term and more recently), justices do not always rule as expected.[33] This can become even more prominent when a justice is later appointed as chief justice and takes on a leadership role on the court.[34]

Finally, there is a more recent nonconstitutionally based presidential "power" that should also be discussed: the "power" not to be indicted or charged with a criminal offense during the president's term.[35] Why is this a "power?" Even though Congress can investigate a president for improper or even illegal behavior, and if it has the political will, impeach the president for such behavior, Department of Justice policy—not a law and not the Constitution—does not permit a president to be criminally indicted or charged during his or her term(s) of office. Unlike civil cases, the statute of limitations—the time period after a crime is allegedly committed in which the accused must be charged for such a criminal offense—is stayed during the president's term of office. Thus, statute of limitations for a presidential criminal offense (other than, for example, murder or sexual assault of a minor) is likely to expire prior to the expiration of a two-term presidency.[36] This "power" creates a strong incentive for a president who commits such a crime in his or her first term to be reelected. This is because the statute of limitations for such a crime is likely to expire before he or she completes a second term. Isn't it troubling that a president could commit a criminal offense while in office and *never* be held accountable for it?

CONGRESS

TL; DR

- By creating congressional districts to achieve political party objectives, many states make many voters' votes irrelevant. Combined with closed primaries, this results in double disenfranchisement.
- Congressional elections are about money and influence, which is compounded by a lack of term limits.
- Because only one-third of the Senate is up for reelection every two years, a party may retain control of the Senate even when that party does not have (or loses) control of the House of Representatives.
- Political parties and seniority matter in congressional elections and Congress.

- Congressional representatives and senators are expected to, and spend, a substantial portion of their day on party fundraising, not official government business.
- Confirmation of federal judges, especially those of the Supreme Court, has become needlessly politicized.
- Some of Congress's powers, most notably the power of investigation, are not even listed in the Constitution.

CONGRESSIONAL DISTRICTING

As we learned in civics, the House of Representatives has 435 members. The number of representatives in each state is based on the eligible voting population of each state. Because the total number of representatives is fixed at 435, some states gain or lose representatives as a result of population changes reflected in the U.S. Census, which is conducted every ten years. Once the number of districts in each state is determined, the states—not the federal government—determine which voters and locations are in each of those districts, a process called reapportionment.

You might think that this is a formulaic, objective exercise that results in districts that look like squares, or rectangles, or circles, or that they neatly match city or county boundaries. Unfortunately, that is not at all how it's done. "Gerrymandering"[37] describes how some (perhaps even many) districts are determined.[38]

What is gerrymandering? It's determining congressional district boundaries to benefit the in-power political party (or interests) in a state. It results in some pretty unusually shaped districts like:

The nation's most gerrymandered districts

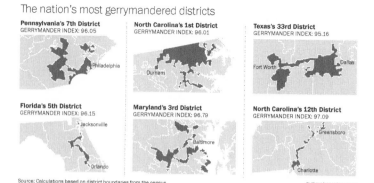

Pennsylvania's 7th District
GERRYMANDER INDEX: 96.05
Philadelphia

North Carolina's 1st District
GERRYMANDER INDEX: 96.01
Durham

Texas's 33rd District
GERRYMANDER INDEX: 95.16
Fort Worth · Dallas

Florida's 5th District
GERRYMANDER INDEX: 96.15
Jacksonville
Orlando

Maryland's 3rd District
GERRYMANDER INDEX: 96.79
Baltimore

North Carolina's 12th District
GERRYMANDER INDEX: 97.09
Greensboro
Charlotte

Source: Calculations based on district boundaries from the census.

THE WASHINGTON POST

Although there are many ways to do this, a common way is to place enough, but much less than a majority, of the other party's voters in districts in which there are a majority of voters aligned with the dominant party. This can result in the nondominant party not having a majority of its voters in *any* district. Another strategy is to place an overwhelming majority of the nondominant party's voters in one district to keep them from diluting the dominant party's voting power in the remaining districts. Both strategies dilute the nondominant party's representation in Congress and result in the distorted district boundaries like those shown above.

By enabling the dominant party in each state to have a greater proportional number of congressional representatives than its overall statewide percentage of voters and the other party to have fewer, this scheme helps a party maintain or obtain congressional majorities. In turn, having that majority increases political power, including the power to name the Speaker of the House and to have majorities in all congressional committees. If you're thinking this is a pure political power grab, you've got the concept down.

However, it's bad public policy and results in We the People having a less representative government. It's a way to disenfranchise voters from the non-majority party in each state, by helping ensure that they will not be able to elect a representative who expresses their political viewpoint.

Gerrymandering and political redistricting sounds so technical (and boring) that it's difficult to get a sufficient number of people in each state to force the state to end this practice. When some try, as in states like my home state, Illinois, the majority political party uses all kinds of legal maneuvering to prevent it from happening, including judicial challenges to state courts with politically elected or appointed judges.[39] What can we do about it? (1) Understanding what gerrymandering is and why it is bad and (2) getting coalitions of voters to pressure the state to put anti-gerrymandering provisions up for a statewide vote, as has been done in at least four states.

One argument in favor of gerrymandering is that it avoids disenfranchisement of racial minorities. The argument goes that if more natural geographic boundaries are drawn, racial minorities will never have enough votes to vote "one of their own" into Congress. That argument is wrong as a policy matter because it creates racially segregated districts. It is also wrong factually. Gerrymandering has been used to disenfranchise racial minorities more than it has been used to enfranchise them.[40] Notably, in states that have ended gerrymandering, racial minority enfranchisement has increased, not decreased.[41]

In states with a closed or semi-closed primary (i.e., one in which independents cannot vote), gerrymandering results in double disenfranchisement in primary elections. In addition to disenfranchising nondominant party voters, it also disenfranchises independent voters by denying those voters an opportunity to choose a party candidate other than the one supported by the dominant party or to support a more moderate candidate of the nondominant party who could better defeat the dominant party candidate in the general election.

CONGRESSIONAL ELECTIONS

Just as is true in presidential elections, congressional elections are about money and influence. First, the money side. Congressional campaigns are expensive and have become increasingly so.[42] Congressional candidates have also increasingly relied on bundlers and super PACs, just as presidential candidates have.[43] Unlike presidents, who have a limited term, neither congressional representatives nor U.S. senators have any term limits. Thus, incumbents continue to build power, through money and influence, with each term they serve.[44]

We'll discuss that more in a little bit, but before we get to that, we need to discuss a special feature of U.S. Senate elections. It relates to the different terms that U.S. senators have from congressional representatives.

As we were all taught in civics, congressional representatives have two-year terms, and U.S. senators have six-year terms. Thus, each congressional representative faces reelection every two years. If senators have six-year terms, why are some senators up for reelection every two years? The answer: staggered terms. Each Senate seat is assigned to one of three staggered cycles, which results in approximately one-third of senators being up for reelection in each two-year election cycle.

But there's a political implication from this staggered schedule:

in each two-year election cycle, an uneven number of senators from each party faces reelection. The practical effect of this is that it makes it much harder to change the political composition of the Senate in certain elections, such as the 2018 election. As depicted below, three times as many Democratic Senate seats than Republican seats were up for reelection in 2018, and the Republican Senate seats were largely in states with substantial majorities of Republican voters.

SENATE SEATS UP FOR GRABS IN 2018

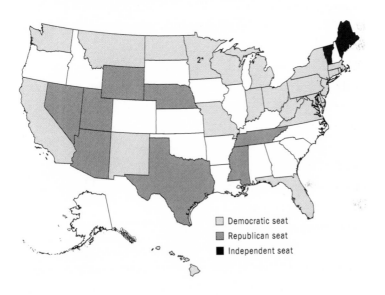

*Included special election to replace Al Franken, who resigned midterm.

In the 2018 election, Congress changed from a Republican to Democratic majority as a result of the so-called "Blue Wave." Even though there was a powerful electoral force behind this shift, the Senate remained Republican. This is because there were not enough Republican Senate seats up for reelection in 2018, and most of those were in "safe" Republican states.

What about 2020? There are thirty-five seats up for reelection of which twenty-three are currently held by Republicans and twelve (or about half) are held by Democrats. This likely provides more advantage than risk to Democratic candidates—not quite the reverse of 2018 but a reverse nonetheless.

There's not really much that can be done about this other than to recognize that it happens and to understand why it does. It would be impractical (and likely unconstitutional) to readjust the cycle to ensure that an even distribution of Senate seats controlled by each party are up for reelection in each election cycle.

THE INFLUENCE OF POLITICAL PARTIES AND SENIORITY

Political parties have significant influence in congressional and Senate elections. This was also demonstrated in the 2018 congressional elections. The Democratic Party successfully returned to the majority in Congress largely as a result of:

- Selecting highly electable candidates.
- Adopting and effectively communicating a simple, clear message that was differentiating and highly appealing to voters—that is, health insurance.
- Effectively targeting and providing financial support in winnable districts.
- Using "real people" in advertisements and minimizing (or eliminating) endorsements from lightning-rod public officials (e.g., Speaker of the House Nancy Pelosi)—even former President Barack Obama was used carefully and judiciously.

That political parties have significant influence is demonstrated by the data. Currently, only three congressional representatives and senators are not a member of either political party, and in the last forty-seven years, only eleven have not been members of a political party.[45] This means that each party has significant control on who runs for and will be elected to the House or Senate. Without party support, a candidate has little chance of winning an election.

Political parties also have strong influence in Congress. Each of the House and Senate and each of the two parties in each chamber select their leaders. The leader of the House is the Speaker of the House; the leader of the Senate[46] is the Senate Majority Leader. Each is from the party that holds the majority in that chamber. As such, each has a number of significant powers—none of which are in the Constitution—but exist as a result of chamber rules and precedent. These powers include committee and committee chair appointments as well as deciding when (and if) certain legislation will be considered by the chamber. Notably, because there are no term limits for leaders in the House[47] or Senate, party leaders accumulate significant power during their tenure by, among other things, positioning their loyalists in highly desired positions and accumulating influence and campaign funds that they can "share" (or not) with their colleagues.[48] It is virtually impossible to unseat a party leader absent four situations: the other party gaining control of the chamber, the leader's resignation, the leader's not being reelected, and the leader's death.

Just as they can reward loyalists with highly desired committee assignments, they can "punish" those who oppose them with undesirable assignments.[49] Committee assignments are not just about obtaining a desired or influential subject matter; some committees have external influence that can be highly lucrative. The broader that influence, the more the chair and committee members are likely to receive (or receive larger) campaign contributions from individuals associated with those companies or interests over which the committee has influence.[50]

In turn, those contributors and other supporters are rewarded with government money through preferential appropriations known as pork barrel projects. In short, a pork barrel project is an appropriation providing money to such a special interest, hidden in a larger, often unrelated bill. According to Citizens Against Government Waste, the total cost of these pork barrel projects in fiscal year 2019 was a whopping $15.3 billion.[51]

All other things being equal (e.g., no public scandals), incumbents have a significant advantage in Congress. First, they are generally able to better attract campaign contributions both individually (especially based on committee assignments) and from their party. Second, they can use official (and publicly paid-for) communication channels to promote what they've done in office, claiming that such communications are merely informing constituents, not campaigning. As they gain seniority and status within the committees on which they serve and/or gain leadership positions within their party, they are positioned to obtain even more financial support both individually and from the party, as well as attract greater media attention.

There are pros and cons to seniority. For the district or state with a senior representative or senator, it can mean greater ability to attract federal spending and projects in that district or state, thus benefiting voters and residents in that district or state. However, it can result in giving smaller districts and states a disproportionate amount of such spending and projects, as discussed above.

Each party's members are each a "caucus" in each chamber that meet and decide how they will support or oppose legislation, as well as political positioning and strategy. When there are independents in a chamber, those members decide which party they will caucus with. The slimmer the majority of the dominant party, the greater influence independents have because their vote is highly sought out by each party.

Perhaps one of the greatest powers of both the Speaker and majority leader is media attention. Although not as substantial as the president's, it is still significant. Successful Speakers and majority leaders have used this power well and often.

POLITICAL ACTIVITIES OF REPRESENTATIVES AND SENATORS

One of the largely unknown aspects of a House member and senator's daily duties has nothing to do with legislative action. Indeed, it doesn't even occur on government property but at party offices near their government offices. That duty? Party fundraising. As revealed in a *60 Minutes* exposé, House members and senators spend hours virtually every day they're in DC at these party offices soliciting campaign contributions.[52] I suspect that this is surprising to most of us, who would expect our elected and publicly paid representatives to be spending most of their time fulfilling their official duties and obligations to us. As with many things, the light of transparency needs to shine brightly on these political activities.[53] Despite the *60 Minutes* exposé, this practice apparently continues unabated.[54]

THE POLITICIZATION OF SUPREME COURT CONFIRMATIONS

The nominations of Judge Merrick Garland by President Obama (to replace the late Justice Antonin Scalia) and the nomination of Judge Brett Kavanaugh by President Trump (to replace retiring Justice Anthony Kennedy) are two recent examples of the politicization of the Supreme Court appointment process. In the case of Judge Garland, Republican Senate leadership effectively blocked Senate consideration of the nomination, making the argument that because of the relative proximity of the upcoming presidential election, the new president (since President Obama was in his second term and could not run for reelection) should nominate Justice Scalia's replacement. Although the facts did not support such an argument,[55] the Senate's strategy, while much criticized, was not only successful in delaying the appointment but was also used to help elect a president from the other party, Donald Trump, by promoting the fact that, if elected, he—and not a Democrat—would make the appointment.[56]

The Kavanaugh nomination was slightly more complicated and requires a greater understanding of the relevant facts and the nomination process. As background, Judge Kavanaugh was a staunch conservative, opposed by most Democrats and many others largely out of concerns that he could tip the balance of the Supreme Court generally and on decisions involving abortion rights specifically.

As the nomination proceeded, it became even more highly charged, emotionally and politically, because of the sexual abuse allegations made regarding Kavanaugh. We may never know the truth about those allegations because of the process and politics involved, which is a shame. If those allegations were true, it is disturbing to say the least that we have a justice of the Supreme Court who committed those illegal and inappropriate actions. If those allegations were not true, it is troubling that even if the principal witness to those alleged actions was truthfully recalling the events as she remembered them, Kavanaugh and his family were subjected to such allegations never having been resolved.

Here is why, I believe, the process and politics related to the Kavanaugh nomination did not serve the best interest of We the People. The reason for this belief, based on these facts, is that the process was used to achieve—on both sides—the political objectives of each party and not to protect two basic rights: Kavanaugh's right to the presumption of innocence and the right of Dr. Christine Blasey Ford, who accused Kavanaugh of sexual assault, to protection from harassment as an alleged victim of a sexual assault. The process, and the participants in the process, utterly failed both Kavanaugh and Ford and deliberately made them pawns in that political process. As the facts that have been made available demonstrate, it appears that the allegations about Kavanaugh first were brought to the attention of Democrat Senator Diane Feinstein of California, along with Ford's strong desire to remain anonymous.[57] As the facts also demonstrate, it is clear that that desire was not honored, and it should have been. No victim of a sexual assault should ever have to be subjected to public scrutiny if she or he wishes to avoid such scrutiny, and in no case should such a victim be subject to personal attack. Yet, needlessly, that is exactly what happened. That this was done with the goal of advancing political careers and hoping to influence the midterm elections was a disservice to the citizens of our country.

Here's what should have happened, which would have perhaps still achieved the political objective—though not as forcefully—and likely resulted in Kavanaugh removing his name from consideration.

Immediately after the allegations were raised, the Senate Judiciary Committee should have met, as they are permitted to do, in a closed-door (non-media-coverage) session with appropriate law enforcement officials to obtain the relevant facts and information relating to the allegations. If those allegations sufficiently demonstrated that there was a likelihood that Kavanaugh may have committed sexual assault, the committee should have met with him privately and told him to remove himself from consideration and that if he did not do so, the facts of which the committee were aware would be made public (the committee having already obtained Ford's permission to do that in that event). This would have given Kavanaugh the ability to avoid the public spectacle that resulted, and most importantly, it would have obviated the need for Ford to have been subjected to such public scrutiny. Needless to say, if the facts demonstrated that Kavanaugh could or should have been charged with a crime, the matter should have been referred to the appropriate law enforcement agency for prosecution, and if convicted, Kavanaugh should have been removed from his *existing* position as a U.S. circuit court judge.

This process could have achieved the result of not having Kavanaugh confirmed as a Supreme Court Justice, while also protecting Ford. As we know, it did neither. That is because, I believe, broader political objectives were at play: Republicans were concerned that the midterm elections might reduce their majority in the Senate, and therefore, if a smaller number of Republican senators failed to support the nomination (especially after a Democratic win in the midterm elections), the nomination may have failed, and the president would have to nominate a candidate with bipartisan support. For the Democrats, a withdrawal of the nomination was not a sufficient win. The Democratic win was creating the publicly divisive battle over the nomination to favorably affect the midterm elections—even if they eventually lost, as they did—their fight over the nomination. Although we may never have conclusive evidence of this, this belief more closely aligns with the publicly available facts than any other explanation.

Even if this belief is not accurate, it is abundantly clear and indisputable that the nomination process for justices of the Supreme Court is highly politicized. The goal is not to determine the qualifications of a nominee but to determine his or her alignment with highly charged and politically divisive positions, coming very close to demanding that a nominee give a judicial opinion on a political issue rather than—as we should insist all judges do—rule only on specific facts in a specific case based on the law that exists at the time of the decision. Perhaps there is no better proof of the politicization of the process than what happened after Justice Kavanaugh was confirmed and after the 2018 midterm elections: the investigation ended. If the real issue had been about what he had allegedly done, that issue would have remained in play. However, because the real issue was supporting or defeating his nomination, when that issue was resolved, the matter ended.

SOME OF CONGRESS'S MOST POTENT POWERS AREN'T LISTED IN THE CONSTITUTION

Some of Congress's most potent powers are not even listed in the Constitution.[58] For example, each chamber's power to conduct investigations of the executive branch and the president have proved more potent than the constitutional power of impeachment. This investigative power, especially when one of the congressional chambers is controlled by the opposite party of the president, has been used quite frequently.[59]

Largely, these "investigations" are politically motivated and self-promotional. Rarely have they resulted in any legislation or other action to remedy the alleged wrongful action being investigated, which is the permissible basis for such an investigation. Rather, their goal appears to be to promote political party positions and objectives, to embarrass the president, and in some cases, to raise campaign contributions.[60] Notably, in many of these investigations, the investigating committee members—both Democrats and Republicans—spend more time making statements or asking questions with a clear bias, rather than seeking to determine the facts related to the issue.[61]

THE FEDERAL COURTS

TL; DR

- Although the Supreme Court is the most visible federal court, the vast majority of decisions are made by other federal courts and not reviewed by the Supreme Court.
- The president selects nominees for all vacant and new federal court positions. Nominations are almost always based on ideological positions; however, there is no evidence that the federal judiciary is biased.
- Courts and judges make law—case law—and there's nothing wrong with that.
- A few key reforms would make the judiciary less susceptible to claims of bias or attempts by some to pick certain courts (called forum shopping) to achieve a desired outcome in a case.

When most people think about the federal judiciary, they think only or mostly about the U.S. Supreme Court. Although the Supreme Court is obviously the highest and most visible part of the federal judiciary, understanding the federal judiciary requires an understanding of more than the Supreme Court. Indeed, the U.S. Supreme Court takes only a small fraction of cases each year (between 1 percent and 2 percent of the cases it is requested to take). The vast majority of federal court decisions are made by the ninety-four U.S. district courts and the twelve regional U.S. Court of Appeals.[62]

What is the same about all these courts is that the president appoints their members and that each appointment is a lifetime appointment. Federal judges are not elected and do not have terms. Appointments are made only when there is a vacancy due to a resignation, death, or impeachment, all of which are extremely rare, or if a new judicial position is established.[63]

While we should expect (or at least hope) that judicial appointments would be nonpartisan, this is often not the case. This is particularly true when Supreme Court nominees are viewed as tipping the balance on high-profile issues such as abortion.

For Supreme Court nominees, presidents have more often than not appointed justices who share their political or ideological views. Similarly, for other federal courts, presidents have largely nominated judges based on recommendations from senators and representatives of their own party as well as key influencers within their administration. To be clear, this does not mean that these judges are not competent—quite to the contrary.[64] However, it would not be honest to suggest that the federal judiciary has been appointed without political or ideological considerations.[65]

Indeed, the process has been set up as a political one, even though it need not be.[66] Just as the nomination process is largely political, Senate confirmation of nominees is also largely political. The so-called blue-slip rule allows one or both senators of the state of residence of the nominee to prevent the nominee from being considered. The so-called Thurmond Rule, named for the late Republican South Carolina Senator Strom Thurmond, has been used to prevent the Senate from considering nominations during the last year of a president's term.[67] A recent congressional study demonstrated the influence of political considerations in the confirmation process: the lowest percent approval of nominations occurred when the president and Senate were of opposing parties, the highest when the president and Senate were from the same party.[68] But perhaps no better evidence exists than in the confirmation hearings themselves, which demonstrate that political positions predominate the Senate's consideration of judicial candidates.

Although the nomination and confirmation process may be political, it does not, as some have suggested, result in judges who are politically biased. Although some have attempted to label each of the federal Court of Appeal as either "Republican" or "Democratic" based on whether a Republican or Democratic president appointed a majority of judges on that court,[69] there appears to be no clear, objective evidence of such a bias. Without such evidence, allegations—from either political party or ideology—that there is such bias, unnecessarily undermine public confidence in the federal judiciary.

Two other points: First, we need to eliminate the unhelpful and incorrect statement that the judiciary does not make laws. This is often a shortcut for the argument that the Supreme Court should give almost absolute deference to congressional or presidential actions, only striking down such actions when they are clearly unconstitutional. This position misses the mark because the federal courts' review of congressional or presidential actions is not limited to constitutional deficiencies. Rather, federal courts are required to review compliance of those actions with many laws other than the Constitution. Their role is to determine whether such actions are both constitutional and lawful.

Statements that "courts don't make laws" fundamentally misstates the basis of our legal system. To be brief, there are two principal Western law systems: code based and common law based. In a code-based system, judicial decisions have binding effect only in that particular case. In a common-law-based system—which is what the United States has[70]—judicial decisions are binding in subsequent cases, creating what is known as case law. In deciding matters that are presented to them, the federal courts must consider both the relevant legislative or presidential-made "laws" as well as case law—judicial decisions relevant to the matter. Interestingly, at various times on various issues, both political parties have argued that the judiciary should not make laws and, at other times, that the judiciary needs to follow previous case law.

Second, we have to figure out a way to end politically based forum shopping when someone disagrees with a presidential or congressional action. Right now, based on reality or perceptions, opponents of such an action seek review of that action in a "favorable" court. For example, if a circuit is perceived as "Republican," opponents of a "Democratic" action will file an appeal of that decision in that circuit and vice versa. Sometimes, appeals of the same decision are filed by respective opponents or proponents in different circuits in a race to the courthouse. This only amplifies the perception of political bias in the federal judiciary. Compounding this is the more recent trend of such circuits entering national injunctions, beyond the jurisdictional boundary of that circuit. This rewards politicization of the judicial process and gives too much power to an individual circuit court.

What should We the People expect of our political leaders and the political process to better ensure both a politically unbiased judiciary and to maintain public confidence in the federal judiciary? The answer is actually quite simple: identify and call out any such biases in the process. This could include any or all of the following:

- Having a bipartisan, term-limited judicial nomination, recommendation, and review commission to evaluate potential nominees or identify current lower level federal or state judges as potential nominees when a higher-court vacancy arises.

- Comprehensively vetting nominated judges prior to their first judicial appointment to avoid issues like those that have occurred in recent Supreme Court nominations and updating that comprehensive vetting only from the time of the first vetting to the current nomination.

- Revising the Senate Judiciary Committee nomination process to make it less political. For example, the committee's proceedings should be private, similar to those of the Senate Intelligence Committee. Unlike the selection of our president and members of Congress, the confirmation of federal judges is not one that requires public input. Recent public attention to the confirmation process has focused more on voyeurism around allegedly scurrilous actions of nominees rather than on their qualifications to be a judge.[71] An additional advantage of a nonpublic proceeding is to enable the committee to receive confidential federal law enforcement reports of potential nominees and to question relevant witnesses without subjecting them to the increasing abuses that have arisen from a public process.

- End the practice of asking judicial nominees to state how they would rule on specific issues. None of us should want any judge to have already decided how he or she is going to rule on a specific issue or in a specific case, without that judge having a specific set of facts and a specific set of laws in front of him or her, and making a decision based on those facts and those laws. As important politically as some of the underlying policy issues may be to different groups of individuals in our country, decisions on those issues should come from Congress, not an independent judiciary.

- As responsible citizens, we have a role, too. We should insist that political candidates not attempt to politicize the federal judiciary in their campaigns. Although it would appear that a prohibition on such attempts would not survive a First Amendment, free speech challenge, that does not mean that we have to "take the bait." We, the media, and other participants in the election process should be more diligent in calling out these attempts and calling them out for what they are: attempts to politically influence our federal courts.

- End the practice of federal judicial forum shopping, including limiting the ability of a single circuit court to enter nationwide injunctions.

CHAPTER 3

THE MOST IMPORTANT THINGS YOU NEED TO KNOW ABOUT STATE AND LOCAL GOVERNMENTS

As stated above, it is both beyond the scope of this discussion and keeping things simple and meaningful to discuss each of the fifty U.S. state governments or even to compare them. Discussing the thousands of U.S. local governments would be even more daunting and irrelevant to anyone other than those people living in each of their individual jurisdictions.

Instead, this discussion focuses on the key things we all need to know as citizens to understand how state and local governments work and, with that understanding, to be able to participate in and influence our respective state and local governments.

STATE GOVERNMENTS

There are many similarities between the federal government and state governments. All state governments have three branches—executive, legislative, and judicial—although there are a few meaningful differences about those branches that we will discuss. All state governments except Nebraska have a two-chamber (or bicameral) legislature, and the members of the smaller chamber, generally called the Senate, have longer terms of office, and most state legislatures (thirty-five) do not have term limits.[72]

And, unfortunately, money and influence are, like with the federal government, important to understanding how state governments work; in fact, money and influence may have a greater influence on state governments.

TL; DR

- States have more power than the federal government.
- State governments are less transparent than the federal government.
- State candidate selection and elections are even more subject to control by party insiders than in federal elections.
- Because they lack term limits and because they have smaller constituencies, most state officials accumulate great power with little transparency.
- Most state judges are selected in processes that are even more political than in the federal government.
- Unfunded state government employee pension liabilities are substantial and growing, and we will have to pay for them.

STATE GOVERNMENTS HAVE MORE POWER THAN THE FEDERAL GOVERNMENT

State governments have different but more powers than the federal government. State government powers are different because states are constitutionally prohibited from having many powers exclusive to the federal government—for example, no state can establish its own currency. However, states have more powers than the federal government since the U.S. Constitution reserves all powers that the federal government doesn't have to the states or to the people.[73] These powers, generally, have more day-to-day effects on us, such as vehicle and driver's licensing, educational requirements, and other similar matters.

An unusual twist to states' power is exemplified by California. California has used its size (economic and population) to impose its state laws across the country or even around the world. So long as the federal government does not preempt these laws on matters where federal preemption would not apply, California (and other large states) can lawfully exercise this power.

For example, consider the California Transparency in Supply Chains Act.[74] In 2010, California enacted this law, which requires California companies and companies doing business in California to put disclosures on their websites about whether any of their products or components of their products are sourced from countries in which human slavery or trafficking occurs. To avoid making a false statement, these companies have to undertake investigations to determine the origins of all products and components of the products the company sells or purchases not only in California but anywhere in the United States or globally.[75]

More recently, in 2018, California passed the California Consumer Privacy Act, which allows consumers to require companies to disclose information about data collected from those consumers and allowing consumers to limit collection and use of that data. The law applies not only to California companies but also to any company that does business in California or collects and uses data of a California resident. As a result, the law will apply to virtually any business (the only notable exception is for very small companies with annual revenues less than $25 million).[76] As a result, companies are left with a dilemma: implement the act for all their customers, not just California residents, or set up a two-tier system, one that applies to California residents and one that applies to all other residents.[77] Because of the cost and compliance issues in setting up a two-tier system, most companies have implemented a single, nationwide system that complies with California requirements. This is how California uses its size and influence to make laws that apply in all states and, in some cases, internationally.

STATE GOVERNMENTS ARE LESS TRANSPARENT THAN THE FEDERAL GOVERNMENT

First and perhaps most importantly, there are fewer, less-experienced media outlets to cover state governments than exist for the federal government. Although there are several exceptions, including ProPublica, even it cannot cover all of the significant issues involving any one or certainly all state governments. Some of this is us: there is both less interest and more trust (comparatively) in our state governments[78] even though we know less about our state governments than we do the federal government.[79] Thus, as the media continues to focus on eyeballs and dollars, most of the information about government that we receive is about the federal government, not our state governments.[80]

Relevant information about important state government matters are also not readily provided in a meaningful way.[81] Most governments do not provide ready access to this important data and information, including government expenditures, and others fail to meaningfully respond to requests for such information, under Freedom of Information Acts or other similar statutes, requiring disclosure of this information.[82] Open Meeting Acts (also known as Sunshine Laws), which require states (and local) governments to conduct meetings in public, are not robust in many states, and there are so many exceptions in other states that they do not provide the public (i.e., us) with meaningful access to or participation in our own governments' decisions.[83]

Finally, some important matters are still resolved in closed, back-room meetings. For example, recently here in Illinois, a replacement for a state representative who resigned after being charged with bribery, was done by party leaders in a closed-door process in which the resigning state representative had the greatest percentage of votes to determine the outcome![84]

STATE CANDIDATE SELECTION AND ELECTIONS ARE EVEN MORE SUBJECT TO CONTROL BY PARTY INSIDERS THAN IN FEDERAL ELECTIONS

How state candidates are selected is different from how federal candidates are selected. There are no "caucuses"; there are six different types of primaries including, in four states, a "top-two" system in which the two candidates who secure the most votes, regardless of their party, make it to the general election. These practices often limit candidates to party insiders and, in the case of "top-two" systems, often result in ensuring that only candidates of the majority party can be elected to statewide positions. As noted above, in some situations, nontransparent weightings and party-insider-only slating meetings give party insiders or incumbents a virtually unchallengeable power in selecting candidates.

MOST STATE ELECTED OFFICIALS ACCUMULATE GREAT POWER WITH LITTLE TRANSPARENCY

Most state government officials do not have term limits,[85] including most state legislators. As a result, these individuals can accumulate substantial, lifetime power that is more potent than that of statewide elected officials without—and this is the key point—any statewide accountability. They merely have to obtain a majority vote within a narrowly defined legislative boundary, reflecting a small minority of statewide voters, to maintain their seat and power. These legislative leaders (or their operatives) maintain that statewide power by controlling their districts. In some cases, that "control" includes patronage, electoral misconduct, and even threats.[86]

STATE GOVERNMENTS ARE MORE CORRUPT THAN THE FEDERAL GOVERNMENT

Money and influence are even more a part of the executive branch of state governments than in the federal government, and so, too, is corruption.[87] Eighteen U.S. governors have been convicted of crimes involving, or occurring during, their government service, and one additional governor is currently under indictment.[88] Overall, integrity scores for state governments are poor.[89]

Nepotism (hiring relatives) is not prohibited at all by several state governments, and in those states where it is restricted, most restrictions have substantial loopholes (e.g., they don't apply to the legislature or only to certain agencies or positions).[90] Where permitted, nepotistic hiring or awarding of contracts is not publicly disclosed in a meaningful way. In addition, legislators without restrictions on outside employment[91] can (and have used) their outside employment to help fund their political campaigns and expand and entrench their political power.[92]

MOST STATE JUDGES ARE ELECTED IN A PROCESS THAT IS EVEN MORE POLITICAL THAN IN THE FEDERAL GOVERNMENT

Most states elect judges and just under half elect judges to their highest court.[93] In eight states, including several large states such as Illinois, Texas, and Pennsylvania, judges to the highest court are elected in partisan (political party) elections. Even though there are arguments both for and against the election of state judges, the election, especially a partisan election, of state judges can lead to perceptions (if not the reality) of biased decisions on many important state issues. One of those issues is having the final word on state legislative redistricting or election issues,[94] which can benefit the party in power and can be affirmed by a court comprised of a majority of justices of that same party.[95]

UNFUNDED STATE GOVERNMENT EMPLOYEE PENSION LIABILITY[96]

Of all the big issues facing state governments, the one with the greatest potential (or in some cases, current) financial impact on us is unfunded government pension liabilities. The issue is little understood and difficult to solve as a result of a number of politically imposed legal (and even constitutional) constraints.

First, there is the issue of the amount owed for state government pensions, including post-retirement benefits, such as healthcare. To understand the issue, you need to understand the difference between a defined benefit retirement and defined contribution retirement. Defined benefit plans, which are uncommon other than in government, are based on a system under which, at retirement, you receive a specific, guaranteed monthly or annual amount, known as a defined benefit, generally for life. Defined contribution plans, which are what the vast majority of other employers provide, is based on a system under which you and/or your employer contribute a specific amount toward retirement and that accumulated amount and any earnings on that amount are available to you at retirement without any guarantee of a specific annual payment.

In addition, other than in government, the vast majority of employers no longer provide post-retirement healthcare. You are responsible for your own healthcare costs or when eligible for Medicare. For the limited number of nongovernmental employers who provide post-retirement healthcare, that obligation ends or becomes supplemental to Medicare when the retiree becomes eligible for Medicare. Most state government retirees continue to receive employer-paid post-retirement healthcare, regardless of whether they are eligible for Medicare, at no or little cost.

The point? Unlike the rest of us, state government retirees receive guaranteed pension benefits and post-retirement healthcare at no or low cost.[97] Moreover, since the amount of these pensions is based on earnings in the last or last few years of employment, pensions are manipulated higher by providing employees one-time salary increases in the last years of employment[98] or by allowing final-year-of-employment payout of sick time accumulated over decades of employment.[99] If a state employee has also been an employee of a different unit of local government or, in some cases, of a government employee union, that employee may be able to collect a pension from each such entity, called double dipping or triple dipping.[100] The resulting accumulated lifetime pension liability can be enormous.

And how does this accumulated liability get funded? Some portion of the liability comes from employee contributions and/or from contributions made by their employing government entity. Too often, though, the combined contributions fail to fully fund the accumulating liability. Who pays for the shortfall? We do, through taxes and fees.

But if only the story ended there…It doesn't.

To close budget gaps, many state governments (local governments, too) have done one or two things to make this problem worse. First, many governments just simply don't fund their anticipated pension liabilities. That is, if they need $500 million to pay for the anticipated pension liability and don't have it, they contribute something less, or not at all, to this liability so that they can balance their budgets. But that liability is still there, and it is still accruing. Second, some governments not only don't fund their anticipated liabilities but also use funds previously used to fund these liabilities for other expenses. No new monies are contributed and previously contributed amounts are diverted, which causes the unfunded liability, the debt each of us are on the hook for, to build, and build, and build.[101]

This gap is so significant that states that have these liabilities are now spending up to a quarter of their budgets on state employee pension costs.[102] That is, twenty-five cents of every dollar you pay in taxes or fees are going to state government employees' pensions and post-retirement benefits.

But that, unfortunately, is still not the end of the story.

If state pensioners receive more benefits than the rest of us, why not reduce those benefits? We can't. In virtually every state, these pension obligations are treated as a contract that can't be broken, so the liability is there for all current government workers.[103] In some states, it is a constitutional obligation—that is, these payments cannot be reduced as a matter of constitutional law. Yes, that is as true as it is absolutely amazing. Those of us who are not government employees do not have such ironclad protection of our pensions, do we?

What about changing it for new state employees? The problem is that many state employee unions resist creating a two-tier pension system that would divide their members. Thus, rarely, if ever, has such a prospective solution been created that would meaningfully reduce the growing state government pension liability.

The result: we pay now and we'll pay even more later.

LOCAL GOVERNMENTS

TL; DR

- Although local governments are closer to their citizens, they can be the least transparent.
- Local elections are less competitive than state or federal elections, with little or no meaningful public nomination process.
- Local government officials are not always professional, and even in well-funded local governments, compliance and ethics remain as significant issues.

In addition to several of the points above, including unfunded pension liabilities and lack of term limits, these are the three additional things you need to know about local governments:

ALTHOUGH THEY ARE CLOSER TO THEIR CITIZENS, THEY CAN BE THE LEAST TRANSPARENT

Local governments can be more transparent than state governments because they broadcast meetings over local, public access channels. However, on other measures of transparency, local governments come up lacking.[104] Among other reasons, not all local officials are familiar with, or effectively trained in, open meeting requirements. We tend to trust local governments more than other governments, and it takes a lot of time and effort to be involved in all important local issues, because it requires directly reading and assessing confusing or incomplete information, unassisted by media or other sources that track and report on local government issues. There is also a lack of transparency regarding local officials' actual or potential conflicts of interest, despite some states' disclosure requirements.

LOCAL ELECTIONS ARE LESS COMPETITIVE THAN STATE OR FEDERAL ELECTIONS

In many local elections, other than in major cities, there is often not a set of competitive candidates for each office. In some cases, the nominating process is done by nonelected caucuses, which nominate a slate of candidates that virtually guarantees their election and that have little or no accountability to residents.[105]

LOCAL GOVERNMENT OFFICIALS ARE NOT ALWAYS PROFESSIONAL. COMPLIANCE AND ETHICS REMAIN AS SIGNIFICANT ISSUES.

Conflicts abound in local governments. For example, many appointed local boards and commissions are comprised of members with vested interests in the subject of their regulation,[106] and those on these boards and commissions tend to go along with individual members' desires on a particular issue or project to avoid retribution on their positions on another issue or project. Supervising officials have limited ability (especially in nonpaid positions) to exert appropriate supervision over government employees who can fail to do their jobs, or in the worst cases, extort millions of dollars from local government funds. In many cases, state statutes and local ordinances provide incredible amounts of discretion to these officials. As a result, these individuals are unlikely to get caught until the amounts become so substantial or outside investigators are brought in.[107] Most of these issues, many of which could be viewed as incompetence as opposed to deliberate malfeasance, are hard to identify and require citizens to have specialized knowledge and time to obtain and review government documents.

CHAPTER 4

THE INFORMATION WE NEED TO FULFILL OUR DUTIES AS CITIZENS

What has become increasingly frustrating in fulfilling our duties as citizens is that we lack the information we need to properly exercise those duties. But how could this be? In the current information age, we are bombarded with information from numerous sources. With the internet, we have never had so much access to this amount of information.

The issue is not the *amount* of information to which we have access but the *relevance* and *reliability* of that information.

As a very wise tax professor I had the pleasure of having at Georgetown, the late Professor Marty Ginsburg, often said as a guide to determining taxability, "Follow the cash." That advice is sound, not only for determining taxability but also for understanding government and politics. Since we know that money and influence are so important in political and governmental actions, information about money and influence is highly relevant to understanding those actions and therefore allowing us, We the

People, to make determinations about the political and governmental actors who represent us.

If we could easily learn who is providing campaign or other monetary sources to a candidate or officeholder, that knowledge could help us better understand what is behind the actions of that candidate or officeholder so that when we exercise our right to vote, our right to protest, and so forth, we can do so more meaningfully and effectively. Similarly, if such information were to be readily and easily available and made relevant, it would be likely that it would deter such candidates or officeholders from making decisions that benefit those donors or influencers and more likely to make decisions that benefit the rest of us.

You might say that information is already available. For example, you can search the Federal Election Commission website and find donor information, and some similar state websites provide similar information. That is correct: those websites contain a large quantity of data, but as presented (whether deliberately or inadvertently), it is neither relevant nor reliable. Here's why.

It is difficult to actually get to that information. To get that information, you would have to know where it is housed. It's not on a site called Political Contributions. You have to know who regulates political contributions for federal candidates: the Federal Election Commission (FEC). Once at the FEC website, you'd have to figure out how to search for the information. To meaningfully search for that information, you'd have to know how the records are kept. You'd have to know that some contributions are given by groups or entities that may not identify who is behind that group or entity, so you'd then have to discover that on your own. Yet, even if you did that, you still wouldn't have all the information you need. For example, let's say we wanted to know all contributions made by a corporation through its officers and employees. We couldn't find it. At the federal level, corporations can't make a direct contribution to a candidate; so instead, their officers, directors, employees, and their spouses do. But, of course, the records aren't kept by the name of the corporation but by the name of the individual officer, director, employee, or spouse. You'd have to know that all those people were associated with that corporation to be able to find out how much that group of individuals contributed to a campaign. The same problem applies for union members or any other special interest group.

Did you know all of this? Probably not.

If you were that sliver of people who did, have you ever done this type of analysis for any candidate? For all the candidates for whom you are entitled to vote this election? Any election? All elections?

Of course not. And that's what candidates and political officeholders are counting on. Yes, they can say that all that information is made available, but it's neither relevant nor reliable because it doesn't provide the information we need to know: what special interests are contributing what amounts to which candidates and officeholders.

We the People need a single source that is widely known with that data already compiled. Without it, we don't have the information we need to make important decisions. Without it, candidates and officeholders are able to hide the financial influence that special interest groups are providing to them.

We need a dashboard that shows for each candidate and officeholder the total that each special interest group and their affiliated entities and individuals contributed to each candidate, and we need a pie chart showing these special interest groups by type. We need to be able to follow the cash.

We also need a way to follow the influence. How can we do that? It's actually relatively easy. To influence, you have to deliver a message about what you want to influence. Messages are delivered in person, over the phone, or in documents (including letters, texts, emails, etc.).

Let's require every officeholder to have a record of all such messages. We could start with a properly recorded calendar that identifies how each officeholder (and his or her staff members) spent his or her day, including meetings, calls, and so on. That would be highly illuminating. Since We the People are paying the salaries of these individuals and they work for us, it's not much different than an employer asking for similar information for their employees.

This type of record, which would include every type of communication with an officeholder, is not at all unprecedented and could easily be implemented. For example, with some federal (and some state) agencies, those attempting to influence an agency decision must publicly file (often within two business days) a letter identifying such communications, including all attendees and what was discussed.

To avoid this becoming an overwhelming amount of data and to make it relevant and reliable, each officeholder would have to report a summary of such communications monthly with links to written communications or written summaries of such communications, as well as a pie chart of how that officeholder spent his or her time that month.

Such information would be very relevant to us to determine how our elected and appointed government officials are spending their time, time for which we are paying. We could see, for example, that an elected official is spending 25 percent of his or her time with special interests, soliciting political contributions, or whatever. That information would allow us to decide whether we believe that employee or official is serving us or serving special interests. It might even encourage these officials to spend more time soliciting our opinions and meeting with us, rather than those with influence and money.

For sure, there will be objections to this, such as providing information about confidential meetings or revealing information about an official's location that may create security concerns. But if the meetings or communications are truly security confidential, that could be noted as well as the parties in the meetings without revealing any security confidential content—for example, meeting at the White House with senior presidential staff (no other non-security clearance individuals present). And by providing the information in arrears, not real-time access, any other relevant security concerns are also addressed.

Just those two pieces of information would provide us with relevant and reliable information that we could use to determine which candidates we will vote for, which current officeholders are not serving our interests, and how to exercise the rights we have as citizens.

Now, to the media.

The media has also failed us in their increasing conversion to infotainers from true journalists. They have blurred fact with opinion and display constant biases in who they hire, who they have as guests, and how they deliver infotainment. They are at best public relations arms of various political partisans. As a result, not only do We the People not know what to believe or what the facts are, but these infotainment outlets can also be easily manipulated by political candidates to promote their positions, dismiss opposing positions, or dilute the facts and importance of significant issues.

To be fair, there are some emerging and historic media outlets that have remained true to journalistic principles, such as NPR and the newly launched ProPublica. However, they represent only a miniscule presence in the overall media arena, and they are known to only a small percentage of voters. Credit should also go to sites such as AllSides.com, which appear to provide reliable assessments of media bias.

As social media has grown, this problem has only worsened, since everyone can be a "reporter" without adhering to basic journalistic principles. Tweets, blogs, and other social media content are used to report so-called facts that are almost exclusively individual opinions and sometimes complete fabrications. One of the most recent and egregious examples was a so-called investigative news report from a social media user claiming that Presidential Candidate Hillary Clinton was operating a child sex slave operation out of a DC pizzeria. Others joined with additional "evidence." Of course, none of this was true, but it allegedly caused a North Carolina man to drive to the pizzeria with a gun and with the intent of "self-investigating" the allegations.[108]

Allowing anonymous comments on these tweets, blogs, and other social media outlets only exacerbates this problem since there is no accountability for these comments, and comments can be manipulated by large organizations and even foreign countries.

Although we have exponentially more media information than

ever before, that information has become less valuable because it misses two things we desperately need: relevance and reliability. More than ever, We the People need true journalism: fact-based, objective, critical, investigative journalism to help us provide that relevance and reliability, to sort out all the increasingly vast information and misinformation that is available to us. But instead of the news media providing such objective, fact-based, relevant, and reliable information, the news media has provided us with exactly the opposite: spin.

Spin is defined as "a special point of view, emphasis, or interpretation presented for the purpose of influencing opinion."

There is no better or compelling proof that the media information in the United States is spin than the fact that virtually anyone with a screen can clearly associate each of the three most popular twenty-four-hour broadcast information media—MSNBC, CNN, and FOX News—with their "special point of view"—that is, spin—along the liberal to conservative scale.

Stop and reflect on that. The one thing that real fact-based objective journalism should *never* have is a point of view, because a point of view is bias, the opposite of objectivity. But not only do each and *every one* of the three most-watched twenty-four-hour broadcast information media have a clear and undeniable point-of-view bias, even worse, virtually *every one* of us *knows* they have that bias, and we've *accepted that as normal.*

And fact-based journalistic reporting? That's missing, too. Turn on any one of MSNBC, CNN, and FOX, and what is their reporting technique? The vast majority is one of two things: (1) a host that has a clear bias and reports his or her opinion of selective facts, consistent with that bias;[109] or (2) a setup "interview" of purported "experts" that consist of a majority or exclusive panel of so-called experts with a point of view similar to that of the media outlet and, on occasion, a single expert with a different point of view, who is attacked by the host and the majority. Such reporting is so at odds with real journalism that we hardly know what real journalism looks like anymore.

Thus, why should anyone be shocked that the majority of us have little, if any, faith in the so-called news media in the United States?

In an equally perverse result, leaders, including but not limited to President Trump, have manipulated that lack of faith and trust into their own spin, causing more spin by the media and less and less relevance and reliability in helping us sort out the truth from lies, the biased from the objective.

Calling the large media outlets "fake news" doesn't help us get relevant and reliable information. Its purpose isn't to add objective facts to the debate but to deflect from the facts through name-calling and polarization. Labeling all unfavorable news as "fake news" is a device that allows anyone to discredit any fact as "fake" if it does not align with their views by labeling it as such. Instead, if someone believes a news report is not based on facts, that person or entity should rebut that story not with a "fake news" label but with specific facts that demonstrate the reporting they are challenging is not factual.

Unfortunately, We the People have been accomplices (some willingly, some complacently) to this dramatic evolution in journalism. Part is human nature: we tend to believe the news we want to believe and discard the rest as biased. This started in the 1960s with the concept of individualism (something we'll discuss later) and has been alternatively used by both liberals and conservatives to reject facts with which they did not agree. The basic concept is that if the facts don't seem right to me and aren't consistent with my experience, they aren't facts. Or, alternatively, if the *source* of the facts is something or someone that I don't agree with, the facts that source presents aren't true.[110]

Another aspect to this is that many of us like the entertainment aspect of the major media outlets and enjoying seeing the "show" and watching the "fights" that are everyday occurrences on almost every major news outlet. The more we have polarizing arguments, even threats of death, the more we watch, the more we are desensitized to such aggression and divisiveness, and the more polarized we become.[111]

But what can be done about this? A good place to start is to go back to the past: by clearly separating facts from opinions. At the very least, opinions ought to be separately identified as such and not identified as facts or news. We ought also to insist that all reporters of "facts" identify objective, real sources for those facts that can be checked easily. If something is said, tweeted, blogged, or whatever without such a source cite, it should not be allowed to be posted as fact but, as was the case with print newspapers for more than a century, labeled as opinion and put on the editorial or opinion page.

We, individually and collectively, can and should challenge the media industry to do better and to return to true journalistic principles. A few examples:

1. Editors should focus less on what will generate ratings and more on whether the information presented meets long-standing journalistic standards, including lack of bias.
2. Deliverers of news stories need to also challenge themselves

to check their opinions and biases at the studio door, as well as their egos. Their job is not to become the news or be the "star" of the show but to present facts and to let those facts become the "stars."

3. Reporters need to do their homework better and to be more challenging with facts in questioning politicians and policy makers. Rather than arguing and fighting with these politicians and policy makers, they should calmly and unbiasedly insist that these individuals and groups provide factual support for their statements and challenge unsupported factual assertions.

We the People also ought to use critical thinking to draw our own conclusions and to recognize bias in media reports and public statements. This is a lot simpler than it would appear to be. We do this already to evaluate statements made by our friends, family, and communities. AllSides.com has an excellent article on its site, which is helpful for spotting media bias. I'm going to condense these and give examples of how we already use many of these techniques in evaluating everyday conversations we each have.

- Dramatic Words: Dramatic words are not objective; they're usually adjectives and adverbs, and all have emotional charge, such as tirade, mocked, or ranted, and the absolutes of always/never.
- Unsubstantiated Claims/Omission of Source Attribution: Stating something as fact without citing a source.
- Opinions Presented as Fact: Value judgments (good, better, best, bad, worse, worst), conclusory words (suggests, means), false-seed-planting words (may mean, may suggest, possibly).
- Mudslinging/Personalization: Attacking the person and not the idea—for example, "nasty," "incompetent," "Never Trumper," "elite."

- Mind Reading: Attributing thoughts or emotions to a person that they haven't said or expressed. AllSides uses the following CNN example: "Donald Trump's hatred of looking foolish and the Democrats' conviction that they have a winning hand..." What is the source for claiming Donald Trump has such a hatred or the Democrats' "conviction?" How they looked? But looks can be deceiving as to the actual emotions.[112]

- Flawed Logic: Inferring something from a fact that is not necessarily true. An example from AllSides: attributing Hillary Clinton's not shaking Melania Trump's hand at President George H. W. Bush's funeral as a snub, even though there was no proof that Melania extended her hand to Hillary or was otherwise in arm's reach. Interestingly, the same article noted that Melania waved in Hillary's direction and Hillary awkwardly and bitterly nodded back. How does one nod "bitterly?"

- Omission and Placement: Failing to include the other side of the story or issue or all relevant facts, or failing to cover newsworthy stories or placing them in a less prominent place in the publication or broadcast.

I'll add three others:

1. First, asking what bias might exist from what you're hearing. Why is the person saying this? What is their motivation/what do they have to gain by saying this?
2. Second, put yourself in the other person's (side's) position. Why would they believe this/state this/act this way? Is there a reasonable explanation?
3. Third, and perhaps most important, is what the other person or other side is saying now consistent with what they've said before? One of the best ways to spot a lie is inconsistency.

As citizens, We the People, each of us, has the responsibility to critically and unbiasedly assess information about our government and its leaders and to determine what of that information is fact based or not, even and especially when we might be tempted to believe that information without adequate factual support because it aligns with our beliefs and positions. Even though finding the facts in the increasing amount of spin is becoming harder and harder, facts matter, and it's up to us to find them.

SUMMARY AND ACTION ITEMS

US (WE THE PEOPLE)

- Understand the effect of money and influence on U.S. elections, but don't let it discourage you. We have the power to change this.
- Don't contribute $3 to the Presidential Campaign fund since it hasn't and won't provide meaningful public funding of presidential campaigns.
- Understand the importance of voting. Don't let polls or a feeling that "it doesn't matter" discourage you from voting: your vote matters.
- Understand that electoral votes, not popular votes, determine who wins the presidential election. Because of that, focus on polling information from battleground states whose electoral votes will determine the election outcome and ignore national polling, which won't.
- Understand "gerrymandering" and support efforts in your state to change redistricting to be nonpartisan.
- Advocate for term limits for all elected officials.
- Learn more about your state and local governments. Many are trustworthy, but given significant lapses in oversight, ethics, and training, don't assume they are working in your best interest. Don't assume that caucus-endorsed candidates are always the best choice.

- Do a better job of assessing information from the media and political advocates:
  - Is the information a fact or opinion?
  - Is factual information supported? Is that support accurate, credible, and unbiased?
  - Is the information balanced? Does it present the opposing viewpoint?
  - Does the information contain dramatic, emotionally charged words?
  - Does the information attack a person rather than the person's position?
  - What is the source's motivation? Why would they say this? Do they have something to gain from providing this information?
  - Are there logical or factual inconsistencies in the information?

GOVERNMENT LEADERS AND OFFICIALS

- Provide more relevant and reliable information about election contributions but not limited to aggregating donations based on individual contributor's affiliations.
- Provide relevant and simplified information about how leaders and officials spend their time and with whom they are communicating. Focus more on serving constituents than raising money.
- Depoliticize judicial nomination, selection, and confirmation processes.
- Spend our money (and your time—since we're paying your salaries) serving us, not major campaign contributors and influencers.
- Stop labeling information you don't like as "fake news," and stop attacking journalists personally. If you have facts to demonstrate a journalist is presenting incorrect information, provide facts to correct that information.

MEDIA (ALL TYPES)

- Clearly delineate fact from opinion.

- Screen content you present using long-standing journalistic standards.

- Let the facts and information be the stars. News presenters should check their opinions, biases, and egos at the door of the studio or newsroom.

- Do your homework, and do a better job challenging and questioning statements and actions of politicians and policy makers. Focus on the facts; don't engage in personal attacks.

PART II

THE SIX PRINCIPAL CAUSES OF LACK OF CIVILITY IN POLITICAL DISCOURSE

CHAPTER 5

INDIVIDUALISM

As the late Senator Patrick Moynihan said, "You have the right to your own opinion but not to your own set of facts."

The belief that facts are only facts if they align with an individual's opinion—that is, each of us can have our own set of facts—is the concept of individualism.

Throughout history, there have been times in which political leaders and those aligned with them have used a variety of tactics, usually based on fear or ego gratification, to cause groups of people, including entire nations, to substitute opinions as facts and to act on those opinions as though they were fact.

This was exactly how Nazi Germany turned an entire country against a race of people, it is how the United States came to jail American citizens of Japanese heritage, and in a nonpolitical context, how now admittedly false data persuaded highly intellectual Americans that vaccinations caused harm to their children, resulting in the resurgence of highly communicable diseases that had been declared extinct.

Some part of this is human nature. We tend to accept statements of purported facts that align with our beliefs and to reject those that don't align with our beliefs, known as confirmation bias.

Second, when someone tells a lie but keeps repeating it, we tend to believe it.[113] This phenomenon even has a name, the illusory truth effect. Indeed, Adolf Hitler is attributed with saying, "If you tell a big enough lie and you tell it frequently enough, it will be believed." Part of the reason for that is that we tend to believe that someone would not tell a *big* lie unless it were true, and if they repeat it, it must *really* be true.[114]

More recently, the internet and other social media outlets have been used to spread demonstrably false information that is perceived as true based on its being on social media: "It must be true; I saw it on the internet."[115]

The media, whose purpose we thought was to help us ferret out the truth, has also largely failed us. As discussed above, one of the subtle ways this occurred—without even being able to pinpoint it to a precise time—was removing previously well-established labeling of facts from editorial opinion.

How did we get to this point, and how do we go back to disassembling facts from opinion?

You will note that in the preceding sentence, I used "we" twice. That use is deliberate. We the People not only have the power to change this situation, but we are also the only people who can change this situation.

For sure, other people and entities may share culpability for this comingling of fact with opinion, but we have allowed it to occur and keep occurring, both by action and inaction. In some cases, we have allowed ourselves to reject obvious facts because they did not align with our beliefs, without doing the work to determine whether those facts were, in fact, true, and being open to modify our beliefs to align with those demonstrably true facts. In other cases, we have refused to challenge others who assert opinions as facts because we liked those individuals or were aligned with their political or other viewpoints.

We can no longer do this.

Opinions are not facts, and facts are not opinions. Facts do not exist based on whether we believe or accept them. There are only one set of facts, not multiple, individual sets of facts. Facts are objective, verifiable, and documented. And facts matter.

CHAPTER 6

SUPREMACY

One of the greatest assaults to civil discourse is the growing trend of supremacy. Simply stated, supremacy refers to an individual or group believing that its opinions and "facts" are superior to any other individual's or group's facts that are inconsistent with that position. It goes beyond mere "individualism"—that is, I have the right to believe my own facts. If it stopped there, everyone would have the right to believe his or her own facts and no one's beliefs would be superior to another's. The idea of "supremacy" is that I have the right to my beliefs *and* my facts and those beliefs are superior to yours. Indeed, it goes ever further because not only are my beliefs and facts superior to yours, but you also no longer have the right to assert your beliefs or facts if they are different from mine.

Stated as such, this position sounds both extreme and an unconstitutional denial of others' free speech rights. But that's exactly what it is and why it is so dangerous.

Two examples demonstrate this in action today.

First is the increasing trend on college campuses to deny opposing viewpoints or facts from speakers, and even from professors, under the guise of "safety." The theory goes like this: I have the right to my beliefs and facts; beliefs and facts that are inconsistent with my beliefs and facts make me uncomfortable and not safe; I have the right to be safe; therefore, you may not express beliefs or facts that are inconsistent with my beliefs and facts. What is particularly troubling about this bizarre phenomenon is that it has actually been accepted at institutions of higher learning that are designed to expose students to varying viewpoints and to allow debate and discussion—civil debate and discussion—of those different viewpoints. In some cases,[116] this theory is even used to justify violence, verbal and physical, against speakers with a different point of view.

Second is the trend that my beliefs can limit another person's behavior and control their actions and words. This is particularly true of religious beliefs. If we critically think about debates of some controversial issues in the last half century, we will realize that those debates were about trying to impose a set of religious beliefs on everyone regardless of their beliefs. Some of these issues have been (and remain) extremely controversial and highly emotional. Unpacked, they demonstrate that their basis is supremacy. For example, laws that banned interracial marriages were based on stated religious beliefs of some (perhaps even a majority) of U.S. citizens. The same could be said of same-sex marriage laws and even abortion laws.[117] The logical essence of these positions was: my religious belief is X, that religious belief is superior to any other belief, so that belief has to be imposed on everyone even if they are not part of my religion. Like the campus speaker example above, this "logic" has been used to prevent any civil debate and discussion of these issues and, in some cases, to justify verbal and physical violence against those with a different point of view.

The problem is that under our Constitution, I cannot impose my religious beliefs on you, nor can you impose your religious beliefs (or lack of religious beliefs) on me. Nor can religious beliefs be used to justify objections to safety and health issues, such as the anti-vaccination proponents who use religious beliefs to avoid getting vaccines. One cannot endanger the physical health of another based on religious beliefs,[118] and religious beliefs cannot be used as a way to diminish any other person's rights.

Even more recently, clashes between the far-left Antifa and the far-right white supremacist groups tragically demonstrate the principle of supremacy that undermines civil discourse. Because each side believes that its position is the only correct one, it must assert that position almost to (and as demonstrated in Charlottesville, Virginia) the point of death.

The First Amendment protects virtually all speech except for very narrow exceptions: where the speech itself is a crime—for example, yelling fire in a crowded theater where there is no fire, threatening to kill or injure someone or a group specifically, or defamation. Other than those exceptions, the First Amendment protects all speech, including speech with which one disagrees or even finds appalling or hurtful. To be clear, what the First Amendment protects is the right to speak, to express one's views and opinions, regardless of whether someone else finds it offensive or hurtful. Allowing subjective, individual determinations of what is "offensive" to determine whether speech is allowed at all is at clear odds with the First Amendment and at equally clear odds with the need to encourage differing viewpoints and engage in meaningful, civil debate and discussion.

CHAPTER 7

POLARIZATION/ABSOLUTISM

Polarization and absolutism are perhaps the biggest obstacles to civil political discourse, and unfortunately, we see it all the time. Perhaps most visible is polarization around a particular view of a political party or leader of a political party out of a sense of loyalty or a belief that not doing so represents capitulation to the "enemy"—that is, the other side.

Polarization stems from individualism and supremacy. It always goes like this: I'm entitled to my opinion and my own facts, those opinions and facts are superior to yours, and you either agree with me or you're the enemy. There can be no middle ground.

Recent studies have found that only about 15 to 20 percent of us are actually politically polarized at the extremes of a given position.[119] The rest of us have something called affective polarization in which we remove ourselves from the discussion of political matters because of our rejection of extreme political views. The result is that We the People, who could be most effective in solving the pressing issues that we all face, don't engage in the discussion and therefore in the solution of these issues. *Achieving this disengagement is exactly the strategy of the polarized extremes.*

If we view "politics" as something dirty, something to be avoided, we will not only sit out the debate on these issues (the first objective of this strategy), but we'll also align our voting behavior and beliefs against whatever the extremes label as "political" (the second objective of this strategy). Should anyone try to find middle ground between the extremes, those extremes will personally attack as a warning to others to stay away.

Although both "sides" have done this, President Donald Trump has demonstrated the result of successfully implementing this strategy. Indeed, he stated that he could "stand on Fifth Avenue and shoot someone and he wouldn't lose any voters." The strategy used to achieve this result: tagging and labeling opponents as "political" to avoid focusing on substantive issues or relevant facts, such as "drain the swamp," "anti-American," "political witch hunt," and so forth. These labels have particular appeal when the president's supporters can point to fringe members of the opposite party who make similar statements. For example, *just hours after she was sworn in*, Michigan Congresswoman Rashida Tlaib said about Trump: "We're going to impeach the MF."

This is exactly how the Trump impeachment process played out. President Trump and some of his supporters created their own facts, insisted that anyone who suggested that he had done anything wrong was evil, and that anyone who didn't support him or his positions were equally evil. He labeled the whistleblower as a "traitor" and suggested he or she should be shot. He personally attacked and intimidated any witnesses who presented contrary facts, firing or dismissing several of them after the impeachment proceedings ended. Democrats appeared to be investigating Trump just for the sake of investigating, taking unprecedented attempts to obtain the president's tax returns, the most blatant of which was California enacting a law (since overturned) requiring presidential candidates to release their tax returns as a precondition of being on the ballot. Before the facts came out or even were presented, many Democrats predetermined that the president should be impeached, and many Republicans predetermined that the president should *not* be impeached. This not only gave credence to the president's name-calling and labeling, but more importantly, it also made most of us conclude that this was just another nasty political fight that we'd best stay out of.

Another aspect of polarization is also troubling. It goes like this: you can't be friendly (or even civil) with anyone who is deemed to be part of the "opposition." This view recently reared its ugly head when Ellen DeGeneres sat with former President George W. Bush at a football game.[120] The criticism was immediate and strident.[121] To be clear, all that Ellen did was to sit with the Bushes and to be friendly with them. She did not endorse former President Bush's policies or positions. Let's unpack why Ellen's actions were so "evil": your policies and who you are as a person must be treated the same; if I disagree with your policies, you are evil; and—this is the polarization point—no one should be civil or friendly to you without also being evil. That's quite amazing, isn't it? But it appears to describe—quite precisely and unequivocally—that polarization is a cause of and creates lack of political civility in our country.

I will also posit that this argument is selective and discriminatory. Notably, Michelle Obama's friendship with former President George W. Bush did not earn the former First Lady such scorn and criticism. Nor did the well-documented friendship between the late Justice Antonin Scalia and Justice Ruth Bader Ginsburg (the "notorious RBG"). Is that because we "like" Mrs. Obama and Justice Ginsburg? Why haven't the same people who heaped scorn on Ellen done the same to either of them?

To the contrary, the ability of leaders and people with diametrically opposing viewpoints to come together have led to some of the most prolific and successful joint problem-solving in our country. Two examples: President Ronald Reagan and Speaker of the House Thomas "Tip" O'Neill, and Ann Atwater and C. P. Ellis, whom we'll discuss later.

We need to separate positions from the person. You can have positions with which I disagree and I can still be civil with you. And you can have positions I agree with and not be a person of character. To demand that I shun everyone who has a position with which I (and others) disagree or to demand that I accept the morally unacceptable actions and words of someone with whom I agree is not only wrong, but it is also divisive and leads to the solution of fewer (or no) problems, rather than more.

CHAPTER 8

ANONYMITY

Go online and find any "news" story from any source that allows comments. Pick even the most neutral and uncontroversial story, and you will find hateful and divisive comments—comments that most people would never, ever say to someone face-to-face or write if they had to sign it.

Although it is true that courts have recognized that the First Amendment right to freedom of speech includes the right to anonymity of that speech, that does not mean that hateful and divisive comments should be permitted by social or other media, nor that they should be given equal weight to non-anonymous comments.

First, let's make sure that we understand what the First Amendment says:

> Congress shall make no law respecting an establishment of religion, or prohibiting the free exercise thereof; or abridging the freedom of speech, or of the press; or the right of the people peaceably to assemble, and to petition the government for a redress of grievances.

The courts have interpreted the First Amendment (and similar state constitutional provisions) to mean that the First Amendment applies only to government actors. It does not apply to private parties. Thus, even to the extent that the courts have interpreted the First Amendment to include the right to anonymous speech, that interpretation applies only to governments, not to the media, not to other private parties.

Second, every right in the Constitution has corresponding responsibilities.[122] Even though we have the right to free speech, we also have the responsibility to speak truthfully and to be accountable for our speech. For example, although we have the right to speak freely, if we slander someone, they may sue us and recover damages. Providing unlimited anonymity of speech that is hateful, contains blatant falsehoods, and other situations where such speech would subject the speaker to civil (or criminal) liability should not be tolerated. Moreover, absent a very small set of situations, such as whistleblowers who follow protections available to them, anonymous speakers' viewpoints should be given less or no credibility.[123] And consistent with slander laws, those who repeat those viewpoints should have the same responsibility and accountability for repeating false and otherwise actionable speech.

CHAPTER 9

VICTIMIZATION

Let's face it, we LOVE victim and villain stories. The victim is good and perfect, and the villain is pure evil and must be feared. Most childhood stories have this theme, with some notable exceptions: "Beauty and the Beast," for example, demonstrates the danger of predetermining victims and villains without knowing the facts.

There may be true villains and victims in fairy tales but rarely in real life. There is usually more to the story, particularly when we jump to conclusions without facts.

Perhaps the best recent example of this involves Jussie Smollett, the actor who claimed he suffered a racial attack in Chicago. Immediately, the media and others, before getting the facts and before critically analyzing Smollett's story, immediately labeled Smollett as the victim and Trump supporters as the villains. People who hadn't even bothered to wait for the facts or to even read them when they did followed the headlines and declared Smollett as the victim based on his version of the event and the fact that he was a "double" minority, black and gay. Thus, his story had to be true, right? Conversely, the reports went to a familiar villain,

President Trump, who was alleged to be the cause of this race- and sexual-orientation-based attack, even though the only facts supporting this were that the alleged perpetrators wore a red hat, which we assumed was labeled "MAGA" (Make America Great Again—President Trump's campaign slogan) and what Smollett claimed was said during the attack. There was outrage in the news media about this story, even though the Chicago Police Department (headed by a black male) later determined that Smollett's story was a complete fabrication.

Why did we all get caught up in this story? Part of the reason may be something that Malcolm Gladwell describes in his book *Talking to Strangers*. We tend to give people the benefit of the doubt that what they say is true. This is especially the case when we think, "Who would lie about something like that?" It could also be because the story played to our biases—that is, we wanted to believe what aligned with our values and beliefs. We believe victims, especially victims whom we believe have historically been in a victimized class. Perhaps we also believed the story because others in our social networks also believed it.

What about the villainization part of the story? Why did we jump to that so quickly and vigorously without much proof at all? That's because where there is a victim, there must be a villain, and this story was no different. It was set up exactly to create a victim and villain story. It would not have been enough that Mr. Smollett was attacked randomly. That would have made him a victim, but we also needed a villain, and from the facts, it appears that he knew that.

There was, as there always is in a victim-villain story, the third component, fear: unnamed others who supported Trump would do the same thing, no one was safe in "MAGA country."

Then, as we all know, the story unraveled. It became quite a different story, and then an even weirder one when Smollett allegedly received a special deal from Cook County State's Attorney Kim Foxx based on allegations of political influence. Then, just as Foxx got tagged as a villain based on these allegations, yet another victim-villain story began, attempting to recast Foxx, a black female, as a victim of the white, male-dominated police union leadership, dredging up unrelated victim-villain stories between the police union and Foxx. All short on facts but long on spin. We do so love our victim-villain stories, don't we? Eventually, as the facts started to come out, this whole situation led to the appointment of a special prosecutor to conduct an extensive review of Mr. Smollett and the state's attorney's conduct in the matter, which at the time of this writing remained ongoing.

The appointed victim was now the alleged villain, the appointed villain had nothing to do with the alleged event at all, and there was a new potential villain and a new potential victim. It had all the makings of a TV reality show.

Victim-villain stories are not new.

Bill Clinton, while president, had a sexual relationship with a White House intern and then lied about it under oath. Apparently, it wasn't the first time President Clinton had allegedly done something similar with a subordinate. Indeed, he was being sued by one of those individuals, and it was in that lawsuit, while giving a deposition, that the president lied under oath. (Yes, he also lied—not under oath—to all of us in denying the relationship.)

Then began a complicated docudrama with the villain and victim being different based on political opinion or viewpoint and largely without benefit of the facts. Some of us chose not to believe the victim, not any victim, of Clinton's actions. We did so because of our point of view: we liked Bill Clinton's politics.[124] Instead of focusing on the what (the facts), we focused on the who. Remarkably, without the who, there was wide agreement about what would have happened on the very same set of facts to a CEO of a corporation: he would have been immediately dismissed by the board of directors.

But there was the who.

And if President Clinton couldn't be the villain, who had to be tagged as the villain? The victim, of course. To this day, many still view Monica Lewinsky, the White House intern, as the villain and not the victim. She did something, wanted something, as a lowly White House intern, who caused the president of the United States to have sex with her and then lie about it. The other women were similarly tagged as villains by Hillary Clinton, including calling one of them "trailer trash" and another "looney-toons." Imagine this happening in 2020, with the #MeToo movement. Would there be a different version of the story, a different ending?

This became a much more complicated villain and victim story. Of course, the Republicans seized the moment and began a wide-ranging investigation of the Clintons, with a partisan prosecutor, Ken Starr, leading the investigation, which ultimately led to an impeachment inquiry. Their actions unwittingly gave the Clintons the opportunity to create a new victim and villain story, starring (no pun intended) Ken Starr as the villain and the Clintons as the victims.

We all know how the story ends. It was not a good ending for anyone. Not for Ms. Lewinsky, not for Mr. Starr, and really not for President Clinton or Mrs. Clinton either.

It has especially not been a good ending for We the People. It legitimized and proved the success of the victim and villain story in American politics—a story that is re-created with a different cast of characters repeatedly, with actors switching from one side to another and repeating—unfortunately—the same set of mistakes but the same types of spin to which we remain an audience divided not by a debate of the facts but by polarized partisan loyalties.

The current immigration debate is exactly such a story, a story fueled by fear.

On the anti-immigration side, the fear is not just the fear that the immigrants will cost you your job, lower your wages, make you pay more in taxes, or that an illegal immigrant will take your children's spot in their preferred college. Those are potent fears all right, but the big fear that President Trump and some of his supporters cite to really enhance the victim and villain story is that the immigrants are criminals and they will rape your daughters and kill them. Now, that's fear. Without a doubt, any crime is a crime too many, and no crimes should be tolerated and no criminals allowed to immigrate to the United States. However, this "fear" argument is based on anecdotal information and a solution that doesn't fit the facts or the fear. The logic (or illogic) of this big fear argument is that immigrants will rape or kill you because immigrants are criminals. But the underlying conclusion is simply not true. In fact, you are much more likely to be killed or raped by a citizen of the United States than an immigrant.[125]

The other side of the fear story is the anti-ICE story: that Immigrations and Customs Enforcement is all about hunting down illegal immigrants and separating them from their families in cruel and unusual ways that are un-American.

In this victim-villain story, all immigrants are depicted as blame-less victims and the government, particularly ICE, are the villains. Like the "all-immigrants-are-criminals story," this story is also flawed: not all immigrants are completely blameless victims. Some have not followed the rules and followed the process to become legal residents or citizens. Some of the immigrants are, in fact, criminals. And ICE isn't just about hunting down illegal immi-grants and separating them from their families using inhumane tactics. This side forgets the *C* in ICE, "Customs," and that cus-toms enforcement is a large part of what ICE does. Conversely, let's be clear about who "immigrants" are. Although the political spin and victim-villain story focuses on immigrants from Latin America and Mexico, the facts overwhelmingly demonstrate that most illegal immigration originates not from our border with Mexico or even by vehicle or pedestrian crossings of that or any other border but by airplane from countries across the globe.[126] But in a good victim-villain story, the facts aren't as important as emotion.

Weirdly, each side of this highly polarized debate only helps fuel the other side's victim-villain story. President Trump, using a fear-based approach (try to come to the United States and we'll take your children away),[127] decided to separate families illegally immigrating at the border, giving fuel to the victim and fear story of the other side. The current Democratic candidates added fuel to the anti-immigrant position by all agreeing to not enforce immigration laws and many agreeing to provide healthcare and other benefits to all illegal immigrants—even healthcare benefits that U.S. citizens don't receive.

What about all the employers of these illegal immigrants in this multidimensional victim-villain story? Remarkably, they are nowhere to be found, even though they are likely to have profited from employing illegal immigrants and may have taken advantage of them through unfair or illegal work conditions and practices.

While this spin continues and dollars are wasted on each side's polarized and extreme positions, the politicians have done nothing—for decades—to provide a comprehensive, balanced solution to the immigration issue, choosing instead to spin their victim and villain stories and stoke our fears.

We the People deserve more.

Let's save the victim-villain stories for fairy tales and fables. Let us, We the People, set our course based on objective facts and critical, unbiased reasoning. Let us, We the People, focus on the facts and not the person.

DEHUMANIZATION

Perhaps the worst aspect of our current state of political discourse is dehumanization. Dehumanization is generally regarded as referring to people as animals or vermin, or worse, treating them in that way.[128] Perhaps a better definition of dehumanization in political debate is simpler: any demeaning statement about (or action directed at) a person based on their having a political view, rather than debating that political view.

For sure, there are degrees of dehumanization: threatening someone with death is worse than calling someone a pig. But whether one form of dehumanization is "better" than another form is a pointless debate. So, too, is the pointless (and childish) debate of which side started it first.

The problem is that dehumanization is the slipperiest of slippery slopes: once we tolerate any form of dehumanization in political discourse, we invite all forms of dehumanization and then physical violence.[129]

One of the most horrific examples of this was the Holocaust. The Holocaust didn't start with rounding up the Jews and sending them to the gas chambers. It started with dehumanization: calling Jews "rats" and "vermin." Why do we do this? If an opponent is not human, the principles of morality no longer apply.[130] This dehumanization became normalized in two principal ways: first, those who secretly held anti-Semitic views felt empowered to use dehumanizing words and conduct; second, many of those who didn't share those views became afraid to challenge such language and actions for fear that they, too, would become subject to those dehumanizing words and actions.

It cannot reasonably be disputed that political discourse in the United States has already begun down the slippery slope of dehumanization.

For those who deny that this has occurred, I would ask you to choose any popular website and click on any news story, then go to the comments section and start reading. You don't even have to pick the most controversial story of the day.

I did this today, October 9, 2019. I could have picked one of the highly charged impeachment inquiry stories. But instead, I found a relatively benign political headline on yahoo.com and found the story, "Trey Gowdy to Join Trump Team in Battle against Impeachment by House." Here's what I found in the comments: commenters calling each other a "dunce," "retards," "imbecile," "hateful melt," "Down syndrome has no party affiliation," "inbred Trumptard," "moochers," "spithole," "moronic," "dumbacratard," "Trey has no soul," "clucking chickens," "brain dead," "demented," "moron," and "swamp creatures." And that was just the first page of comments!

You might be thinking, that's just anonymous comments by a small percentage of people. But that's not quite right or complete.

Similar comments have been made for the past several years and are made *virtually every day* by our elected leaders, including the president of the United States:

- President Trump called his former Staffer Omarosa Manigault Newman a "crazed, crying lowlife" and a "dog."
- Former Senator Minority Leader Harry Reid called Donald Trump a "Frankenstein monster."
- New York State Senator Kevin Parker tweeted "kill yourself" to a Republican staffer.
- Democratic State Representative Stephanie Kifowit said on the floor of the Illinois House that she wanted to pump a "broth of *Legionella*" bacteria into the water supply of Republican Representative Peter Breen and his family.
- Bill Mayer called California Congressman Devin Nunes a "ratlike creature" and Republicans "treasonous rats."
- Radio host Alex Jones, in response, called Democrats "the ultimate cowardly sacks of garbage."
- Trump about U.S. Senator Mitt Romney: "choked like a dog."
- Trump about California Congressman Adam Schiff: "the leakin' monster of no control."
- Trump about immigrants: "pour into and infest our country."
- Nation of Islam leader Louis Farrakhan Sr. said he was "not anti-Semite but anti-termite."
- Eric Trump said Democrats investigating his father were "not even people."
- Former Democratic Illinois State Senator Martin Sandoval hosted a golf outing where guests performed mock assassinations of President Trump.
- White supremacist groups called nonwhites a "parasitic class of anti-white vermin" "anti-white anti-American filth" and "animals."

As Charlottesville and the Antifa attacks in Portland demonstrate, dehumanizing words lead to dehumanizing actions including death to the targets of those words.

For that reason, We the People must not tolerate *any* dehumanization—no matter the degree—of anyone. It simply has no place in political (or any other) discourse. Period.

We must end the personal attacks on people of opposing viewpoints, especially when those personal attacks are from those who share our viewpoints. We must return to a norm where we can discuss *ideas* without attacking those who express those ideas, where we can debate those ideas and even say that they are wrong without claiming that because those ideas are wrong, those ideas and the people who espouse them are *evil*.

How did we get here? I think the answer is pendulum swinging. Such pendulum swinging has allowed the extremes at either end of the political spectrum to squash meaningful and productive debate. The goal of the extremes has been to attract enough of us in the middle to join one extreme or the other to give that extreme political power and then normalize that extreme's positions without resolving the underlying issues that needed to (and still need to) be addressed in a meaningful and productive debate.

To avoid picking one point of view, either in time or otherwise, I will focus on a recent event, the 2016 presidential election, to demonstrate how both sides in that election engaged in dehumanizing speech that exemplified or created pendulum swings in the suppression of speech. Again, this is NOT about affixing blame to any one group for this situation but fixing the problem that has existed, continues to exist, and will continue to exist if it is not resolved. If any blame does exist, we all share that blame because we have either engaged in such words or actions or have allowed them to occur without challenge.

The first example is what has been called political correctness. *Merriam-Webster* defines political correctness as "conforming to a belief that language and practices which could offend political sensibilities should be eliminated." The concept that language that is offensive should be eliminated is, by definition, suppression of free speech. That is exactly what political correctness morphed into.

When any person or group is suppressed from speaking, they feel as though they are being deprived of basic freedoms, they resent it, and that resentment builds. This is particularly true when that person or group is viewed or labeled as "lesser" than those expressing the prevailing viewpoint.

Without taking political sides but recognizing cause and effect, this suppression and dehumanization of speech and beliefs is exactly why Donald Trump was elected president over Hillary Clinton in 2016. Indeed, I will posit that Mr. Trump's victory over Secretary of State Clinton was based on a single word: "deplorables," which Secretary Clinton used to describe Trump supporters. That word—a dehumanizing word—labeled anyone who supported a different political viewpoint or ideology as less human than those who supported the opposing political viewpoint or ideology. What it evoked for not only some of those who supported President Trump's political viewpoints but also some of those who did not agree with the morphing of political correctness into political suppression, was that their freedoms were at risk.

For sure, as no one could reasonably dispute, Mr. Trump leveraged that unfortunate comment, which had also exhibited itself in other comments and actions, with a sense of fear around other perceived or actual deprivations of freedoms, to gain support for his election even among people who found him to be vile or offensive as a person. Secretary Clinton lost the election by losing voters in those states who felt left behind in the Obama administration, even among those voters—or perhaps especially by those voters—who voted for President Obama in 2008 and 2012.

At the same time, Candidate Trump injected into the political debate, beginning with his campaign to become the Republican nominee, equally demeaning and dehumanizing language. He made up demeaning nicknames for his opponents and used them repeatedly in attacking them (as opposed to their viewpoints) during the campaign. Perhaps empowered by the revolt against the extremes of political correctness, Trump swung the pendulum to the opposite extreme by normalizing such offensive and dehumanizing speech and physical violence against opponents. If Candidate Trump could say it, and in fact by saying it, it helped him win, it must be okay for us to engage in such speech and actions, too.

With such a pendulum swinging and unleashing of dehumanizing and demeaning speech, those who opposed Candidate Trump perceived it was acceptable to engage in similar behavior. Perhaps the best visual example of this was a magazine cover depicting President Trump as a pig.[131] Notably, each of the dehumanizing and demeaning statements of political figures in the list above occurred during the period since President Trump's election.

As a result of these dehumanizing words, has our nation become more united or solved more of the pressing issues facing us? No. The vast majority would say that we have become more polarized and have solved fewer (and created more) divisive issues.

Why? Because dehumanizing and demeaning speech and actions never unite. They never solve pressing issues; they create them.

We the People have to expect more. We can no longer tolerate either speech suppression in the name of political correctness or safety, nor can we tolerate dehumanizing and demeaning speech. Even though this has been framed as an "either-or" debate, it is not: We the People can insist that we allow all viewpoints to be discussed and heard if we focus on debating the issues and not dehumanizing and demeaning the debaters. We need to call out both those who suppress speech and those who engage in dehumanizing and demeaning speech. Only in doing so can we hope to have a meaningful and productive debate of the many pressing issues we face as a nation.

PART III

REFRAMING OUR DISCOURSE

CHAPTER 11

COMMUNITY/COMMON PURPOSE: THE IDEALS THAT BRING US TOGETHER

One of the best books on communicating with others about tough topics is *Crucial Conversations* by Kerry Patterson, Joseph Grenny, Ron McMillan, and Al Switzler. Indeed, the full title of the book is *Crucial Conversations: Tools for Talking When Stakes Are High*. *Crucial Conversations* is about tough conversations that have three characteristics: opposing opinions, high stakes, and strong emotions. Sounds like most political conversations, right?[132] The entry point for such conversations is defining a mutual purpose that is acceptable to all sides. This enables the parties to frame the discussion to maximize the potential for seeing solutions that align with that common purpose.

You might be thinking there's no way, given the polarizing political debates in our country today, that there could ever be anything in common, let alone a common purpose, between the political extremes. Perhaps. But I truly believe, and the data supports this, that about 75 to 80 percent of Americans share some set of common ideals and purpose. I have referred to this majority throughout this book as "We the People." Even if I'm wrong and it's not 75 to 80 percent but a smaller majority, that's enough to make significant progress on the many pressing issues we face today.

The problem has been that we almost never start with a common purpose. We start with our individual or polarized group beliefs, positions, emotions, villain and victim stories, and underneath all of that, our fears. No wonder our political discourse is dysfunctional and becoming increasingly so. We've got this turned on its head. We need to start with our common hopes, desires, our common purpose and ideals, not polarized positions, spin, and emotional appeals.

Just as we've seen polarization and the lack of common purpose in the last couple of decades, we've also seen at least one major example of common purpose, albeit out of one of the greatest tragedies of the current century: the massacre of more than 3,000 people on 9/11.

Most people, other than small children, remember exactly where they were and how they felt when they first learned the news of the attack and collapse of the World Trade Center Tower in New York City. What we may not remember as well, but what I'd like all of us to recall, is what we felt in the weeks and months after that horrific tragedy. Do you remember?

For a time, we came together as a nation. We shifted our focus back to where it should have been and should always be: on our families—as broadly defined, on our communities and how to unite them regardless of differences. We were proud to be part of something bigger than us as individuals, our democracy, our country. We honored and treasured service, those who bravely and courageously served us on that day, and the service that many of us gave in small ways after that tragedy.

And our national symbol, our flag, was a symbol of unity, not divisiveness, not overtaken by extremists.

What was sad is that it took one of the (if not the) most horrendous tragedies in the history of our country to bring us together.

Some tried to manipulate that unity to define and attempt to align us around principles and values that served their purposes and did not represent common principles and values that we worked on together.[133] Others manipulated that unity into achieving other political or personally motivated goals, such as reducing personal freedoms, supporting hatred and retaliation against certain religions and races, and squelching free speech. Others even appeared to try to financially capitalize on the tragedy.

But that did not mean there weren't unifying principles and values there: principles and values that we've had for a long time, ever since the founding of our country.

Let's begin the search for those values, noting of course that for common principles, values, and purpose to be "common," they have to be established by us, not just some of us.

A principle is a basic idea or rule that controls how something happens or works. A value is a fundamental belief that people have, especially about what is right and wrong and what is most important in life, that controls their behavior. A position is an opinion on an issue. A common principle is therefore a principle or basic idea or rule that is shared among a group of people. A common value is a belief, especially about what is right and wrong and what is most important, that is shared among a group of people.

EXAMPLES

Common Principle: All Americans have the right to personal freedoms.

Common Value: Freedom of speech is a personal freedom.

Position: Some speech should not be protected.

Common Principle: All Americans have the right to personal freedoms.

Common Value: Freedom of religion is a personal freedom.

Position: Individual religious beliefs cannot justify any discrimination.

Common Principle: All Americans have the right to personal freedoms.

Common Value: Freedom of association is a personal freedom.

Position: Traditional families are core values of America.

The problem is that we often start with the position, sometimes—as in the last example—(mis)defining it as a "value"—rather than the true common principle.

What are potential common principles we have as Americans that characterize our nation?[134] I think there are five common principles that most all of us could agree on, taken straight from the Declaration of Independence: equality; the rights to life, liberty, and the pursuit of happiness; and that governments derive their power from the people they govern. Four others are from the Preamble to the Constitution: justice, domestic tranquility, promoting the general welfare, and common defense.[135] To express these in a single word or short phrase, let's use the following:

- Equality
- Life
- Liberty
- Pursuit of Happiness
- Government Serves the People
- Justice
- Domestic Security
- Common Good
- Common Defense

Let's also be clear that if these are our common principles, let's also acknowledge that just like common principles we have for ourselves, our families, and organizations to which we belong, we often fail and sometimes miserably fail to live up to the principles. Just because we have so failed, it does not mean that the principles are wrong: our actions in failing to live up to them are wrong. And it is wrong of us, any of us, to attempt to deny or justify such deviations, especially the most significant deviations from these principles, such as slavery or the Japanese internment, among many others.

We must not allow those failures to permit the misuse or abandonment of the symbols of our nation, including our flag. We must protect such symbols as the embodiment of those principles, however much and especially because we have failed and continue to fail to live up to those principles. These symbols can and should be used to remind us of those principles and identify where we have failed to live up to them. We should never and can never allow a specific political faction that does not represent those values to hijack our symbols. We must fight all such attempts to the same extent we fight for the principles that those symbols represent.

Now, back to the common principles.

I could not find a survey that specifically addressed these principles as opposed to positions presumably derived from those principles. We should have such a survey, expressed neutrally and without dropping down into positions derived from those values. Even though we are unlikely to find unanimity, I suspect we would find consensus.

Let's define each of the common principles above as neutrally as possible and hopefully in a way We the People can agree on:

- **Equality.** Equality means that legal and political rights (and responsibilities) must be applied equally to everyone. These rights include but are not limited to the rights of life, liberty, and the pursuit of happiness.
- **Life.** Each of us has the right to live our life without it being taken away, as long as we don't infringe on other people's rights to live.
- **Liberty.** Each of us has the right to certain freedoms, including the right to think and believe what we'd like to think and believe, and to live our lives without undue interference from others and government.
- **Pursuit of Happiness.** Each of us has the right to pursue happiness as we define it and how we wish to achieve it, so long as we don't infringe on other people's rights.
- **Government Serves the People.** This principle, which is the fundamental principle of this book, is that government gets its power and authority from us and that we ultimately have authority and control over our governments.
- **Justice.** Each of us has the right to be treated fairly and equitably by government.

- **Domestic Security.** We each have the right to safety and security in our persons, homes, and property.
- **Common Good.** The government must work together with us, We the People, to promote our common benefit.
- **Common Defense.** The government works to protect us from common threats to our liberties and freedoms.

Although it is tempting to take these definitions and get to the policy or position for which we would like to advocate, don't yield to that temptation. Focus just on the principle and whether it meets two criteria: is it stated neutrally (without identifying a specific policy or position) and is it something that a consensus of us would agree with. Since each of these represent the fundamental principles on which our country was founded, we shouldn't try to eliminate a principle but to define it in a neutral way to which all of us would agree without expanding it in a way that would advocate for a specific policy or position.

Subject to specific tweaks to these principles and their definitions, most people would agree that these principles are our basic principles. In essence, these principles center on the concepts of individual rights and responsibilities and a representative government focused on helping to ensure those rights. I think that's something most all of us could agree on—and an important start to improving our political discourse.

CHAPTER 12

ACCOUNTABILITY/RESPONSIBILITY

As a Truman Presidential Scholar,[136] I've come to read a lot about President Harry S Truman.[137] Like anyone, like any president, he made mistakes as well as doing a lot of things that were courageous and necessary in a difficult situation and time. For example, President Truman made the decisions to drop the atomic bombs on Hiroshima and Nagasaki, Japan, effectively ending World War II. President Truman also fired extremely popular Korean War General Douglas MacArthur, although Truman knew that doing so would be the end of his political career. However, he believed that his firing was necessary to preserve the constitutional principle of civilian control of the military.

What I admire President Truman most for is not any decision he made but a sign on his desk, which read, "The Buck Stops Here." To Truman, that phrase meant that he took personal responsibility for what he said and what he did, right or wrong, intentional or unintentional.

Taking responsibility and being accountable for one's actions and words is important for each of us and especially important for our leaders. What does taking responsibility and being accountable mean?

To me, it means several things:

- It means, as best we can, *before* we speak or act, we think about how what we are going to say or do will impact others.
- It means, when we've said or done something that has hurt someone else or caused another type of harm or misunderstanding, that we *acknowledge* that harm or misunderstanding *and*—this is the important part—*our role* in creating that harm or misunderstanding.
- It means after we've acknowledged that harm or misunderstanding that, as best we can without creating additional harm or misunderstanding, we seek to make that harm or misunderstanding right.

Nothing about the above is particularly novel or unique. Indeed, we were all taught and retaught, and retaught again those three principles of accountability and responsibility as children, as adolescents, and as adults.

Yet, although on occasion, or for some of us more frequently, we have taken such accountability and responsibility, we have not always done so. It seems that our leaders do so even less.

Why is this true? And why do we not take more accountability and responsibility when we should?

Let me suggest a few potential answers, answers each of us can test based on our own experience. Sometimes we may not realize that we have created a harm or misunderstanding. That's fair, but when we realize it, why do we sometimes fail to take responsibility and be held accountable? It takes courage, courage to admit that we were wrong, both publicly and to the person we hurt. Sometimes even the best of us can lack that courage. We are afraid of what others will think of us, afraid of bearing the consequences of our actions, just afraid.

Those of us in leadership roles, especially as those roles are higher and higher within an organization or in public view, may (wrongly) perceive that taking responsibility and accountability is a sign of weakness, not strength. We refuse to acknowledge that we have done or said something that created harm to avoid being perceived as weak.

Why do we do this? Again, let me suggest potential reasons for this, which each of us can test based on our own experience.

Some of us live under a delusional belief that we are always right no matter what. We will not and cannot admit that we are wrong even when it is so clear that we are. Others of us, and we'll discuss this in the next section, try to place all (or more often some) of the responsibility and accountability on others. We use phrases such as, "S/he made me do it," "S/he started it," "S/he is the person really at fault—look how bad s/he is," and perhaps even the laughable, "The Devil made me do it." For sure, in some cases, maybe even in many cases, there may be shared responsibility and accountability, but that doesn't mean that we can disown our part of that responsibility and accountability.

As commentator S. E. Cupp recently said, for some of us, this is in our DNA.[138] Rather than taking responsibility or accountability, we Deny, Normalize, and Attack. We deny that we did anything wrong or that what we did created any harm or misunderstanding. We normalize our bad words or deeds by saying everyone else is doing the same thing or by doubling down on the same words and deeds that created the original harm or misunderstanding. And then we deflect our own actions by pointing out the bad things that others have said—that is, we attack.

Rather than showing strength and courage and creating positive results, this type of response, especially when done by senior leaders, has an exponentially negative impact. It encourages the rest of us to do the same: if our senior leaders do this, why can't we? Then retaliating in kind becomes the norm since it is perceived to be the only way to counter the other side's failing to take responsibility.

Such a lack of responsibility/accountability has negatively affected our public discourse.

Some examples:

- President Clinton not taking responsibility for his actions related to Monica Lewinsky, a White House intern.[139]
- President Obama chastising Presidential Candidate Mitt Romney for identifying Russia as the primary U.S. foreign policy threat and then deflecting any responsibility for making that comment, which his administration later identified was, in fact, correct.[140]
- Presidential Candidate Hillary Clinton failing to take any responsibility for calling Candidate Trump's supporters a "basket of deplorables," blaming Trump for her making that comment.[141]
- President Trump has yet to take responsibility for any negatively perceived action he has taken, nor has he acknowledged any errors that he has made. Indeed, even after he purportedly took responsibility for the 2018 government shutdown, once the negative effects of that shutdown became apparent,

he shifted the blame to congressional Democratic leaders.[142] When his actions are questioned, including those that led to his impeachment, he describes those actions as "perfect" and attacks anyone who claims otherwise.[143]

There are similar, too numerous to recount examples of other national leaders, including those in Congress, those in state legislatures, and state governors, who also have failed and continue to fail to take responsibility and accountability.

The point: none of these failures to take responsibility or accountability have resulted in improving the tenor or quality of public discourse, nor have they resulted in resolving issues.

The most notable recent example of a politician standing up and taking accountability and responsibility is the late Senator John McCain's response to a comment at a town hall meeting during the 2008 presidential campaign.

Comment: "I can't trust Obama. I have read about him, and he's not, um, he's an Arab."

McCain: "No, ma'am, he's a decent family man [and] citizen that I just happen to have disagreements with on fundamental issues, and that's what the campaign's all about. He's not [an Arab]."

Similarly, we have failed to take responsibility and accountability for our actions in political discourse. We should neither tolerate nor excuse any verbal or physical violence in political (or other) discourse. We must condemn violence or inappropriate comments by candidates or those espousing positions we don't support and those we do support. Today, as I write this, there is yet another example of such failure to take such responsibility.

The event: at a conference of American Priority, AMPFest 2019, a meme-type video was shown depicting a fake President Trump shooting, stabbing, and brutally assaulting members of the news media and his political opponents, including President Obama and the late Senator McCain.

The official statement from American Priority:

> It has come to our attention that an unauthorized video was shown in a side room at #AMPFest19. This video was not approved, seen, or sanctioned by the #AMPFest19 organizers. The organizers of #AMPFest19 were not even aware of the video until they were contacted by the NYT.[144] The first time anyone officially associated with #AMPFest19 was made aware of the video was when the NYT requested comment. We find it shocking that the New York Times would not report on any of the sanctioned events in the article, including our panel conversation LITERALLY condemning political violence while claiming to be upset over a meme that was not sanctioned, shown on stage, or approved. #AMPFest always has and always will condemn political violence. And proof of this was our major panel discussion on this very topic at #AMPFest 19.

Does that sound like American Priority taking accountability or responsibility for something that happened at its conference? Did it expel the attendees who created or showed the video? Did it even condemn them specifically? Rather, it denied responsibility and attacked the media outlet that reported about the video.

Here's what taking responsibility and accountability might have looked like:

> It has come to our attention that a politically violent video was shown at our conference, AMPFest 2019. We strongly condemn the

video, those who created it or who showed it. We have permanently expelled each of those individuals and organizations whom we have identified as being associated with the video, and we will continue to investigate this matter and take appropriate actions against all those involved. American Priority did not authorize nor was involved in any way with that video, and we strongly condemn all forms of and depiction of political violence. We reemphasized this position during the conference and will continue to do so and disassociate ourselves from all those responsible for such heinous actions.

Better? What We the People should expect?

And what about President Trump's reaction to this unauthorized use of his image in the video? Nothing, not even a tweet. Instead, former White House Press Secretary Stephanie Grisham issued the following statement:

> Re: the video played over the weekend: The @POTUS @realDonaldTrump has not yet seen the video, he will see it shortly, but based upon everything he has heard, he strongly condemns this video.

Even several hours after Ms. Grisham's tweet, President Trump did not directly address the video, either in his role as president, as the primary person depicted in the video, or based on his ownership of the Trump National Doral and Resort,[145] where the video was shown.

Instead of condemning the video and any unauthorized use of his image in the video that day (October 14, 2019), he sent twenty-seven tweets and five retweets, including four retweets of Fox News videos. Those tweets included one attacking a political opponent's child and another supporting his former press secretary's appearance on *Dancing with the Stars*.

Sadly, President Trump did not address the video that day or any other day.

We the People must take responsibility and accountability for our actions and words and insist our leaders do so as well.

CHAPTER 13

FOCUS ON FIXING THE PROBLEM, NOT AFFIXING BLAME

Two initial points about affixing blame, political or otherwise. First, some people believe that taking responsibility and accountability is the same as not blaming. That is not true. One can refuse to take responsibility or accountability without blaming someone else, and someone can take responsibility or accountability and blame someone else. Some people think the Truman quote from the previous chapter describes non-blaming, when it is actually about taking responsibility and accountability. As a reminder, it said, "The buck stops here." That's taking responsibility and accountability. If the quote were about non-blaming, it would have merely said, "Don't pass the buck."

Second, we should understand why people blame others. For sure, one of those reasons can be that a person does not accept accountability and responsibility, but there are many other reasons. In politics, a typical reason is defensive: blame avoidance.[146] Such a strategy is based on self-preservation—that is, a de-risking strategy for outlasting a potential crisis. This is why governmental (and other) bureaucracies often have such a tendency to cling to the status quo. The status quo is self-preserving because it avoids risk from acting. This is why "We've always done it this way" is the anthem of the status quo and avoiding the risk of any change.

This defensive blame-shifting strategy both helps maintain self-preservation and puts the person or entity blamed on the defense, requiring them to react and making them the focus. As we saw above, in examples of political blaming, much of it is blame avoidance by attack.

Unfortunately, such blame avoidance by attack has had a remarkably high rate of success in terms of shifting or mitigating self-preservation risks. However, in terms of actually solving the underlying issue, the success rate is low, if nonexistent, because the focus and efforts are on affixing blame, not fixing the issue.

The late Alice Rivlin, who held several senior budget and financial posts in the federal government, wrote an op-ed piece for Brookings in 2018 that argued for politicians to take a "time-out" and commit to a "no-blaming" pledge to correct this situation and return our country to "restoring constructive national policymaking."[147]

It's not only our politicians who need to take a no-blame pledge; it's also all of us. All too often, as is demonstrated by comments on virtually every online article, we engage in similar blame shifting and attack.

Rather than blame shifting, we need to focus on the underlying issue: what can we do to *solve* that?

Think of a dispute you've had with a spouse, friend, coworker, or other person. What happened? Almost always, those disputes start with a blame game: one person identifies the issue and then blames the other for causing that issue. As long as the focus remains on affixing blame, the underlying issue is never solved. Only when you and the other person decide to set aside the blame game and focus on the issue does the issue get resolved.

The problem in politics is that the blame game almost always never ends, and therefore, the relevant policy makers never resolve the issue.

A recent example is gun violence in the United States. I think we could all agree that it is a significant issue that needs to be resolved. But we haven't solved it. The reason is a multidimensional, multiparty blame game. One side blames the issue on people having guns; the other side blames it on mental issues or even that we need more guns to prevent gun violence. Each side goes to its corners with its familiar arguments. The part that is just sad is that the overwhelming majority of us, demonstrated by repeated and conclusive polling, support actionable solutions to help with the problem, including enhanced background checks, prohibitions against certain dangerous individuals from owning guns, and so forth. Because of the continued blame game, none of those potential solutions have been enacted. Each side locks into extreme positions that lack majority support and refuses to enact solutions that We the People support. Those extreme positions are then used by the opposite side to blame the other side for the problem and a host of other speculative harms and injustices, and the blame game continues. We'll discuss this issue more in part 4. For now, suffice it to say that the multidecade issue of gun violence in this country will not be solved until we can move past affixing blame and work on fixing the problem, reflecting the overwhelming consensus of We the People.

CHAPTER 14

COMPASSION AND CONSIDERATION: RE-HUMANIZING DISCOURSE

I'd like to share two stories to start this section.

The first story is from 1942. The United States entered World War II after the Japanese attack at Pearl Harbor. Anti-Japanese sentiment resulted in actions directed at Japanese Americans, especially those living on the Pacific Coast of the United States. At first, the restrictions were focused on taking away their weapons and cameras, but it soon resulted in an executive order, signed by Democratic President Franklin D. Roosevelt, requiring these Japanese Americans to leave their homes and be interned in "camps."

The first such detainment and internment of Japanese American citizens occurred on Bainbridge Island, Washington, a Puget Sound island off the coast of Seattle. Unlike some other areas with Japanese American populations, the Japanese Americans living on Bainbridge Island were well integrated with other cultural and ethnic groups. Although their non-Japanese neighbors could not prevent the detention and internment of their Japanese American neighbors, in many cases they helped preserve their property and welcomed them back at the end of the war. Some of these individual stories are poignantly told on a memorial on Bainbridge Island.

The second story is from 1971. It is the story of two polar opposites. It is the story of civil rights activist Ann Atwater and a Ku Klux Klan leader, C. P. Ellis. These two seemingly polar opposites came together—albeit reluctantly—not only to solve an important, divisive issue in their community but, over a lifetime, to show the power of constructively engaging with those with whom we disagree—particularly, but especially, with those whose positions we find abhorrent. Core to their doing so was getting to know each other as people and recognizing they shared similar human concerns. Indeed, Ms. Atwater and Mr. Ellis became such close friends that Ms. Atwater delivered the eulogy at Mr. Ellis's funeral.

Contrast those stories with the many examples today where those different from us or our political views are attacked—physically and verbally—merely because of their race, beliefs, or policy positions. There are so many examples, including but not limited to the 2017 protests at Charlottesville, Virginia, attacks at various political rallies during the 2016 presidential campaign, protests to prevent and denounce campus speakers, and physical and verbal clashes in Portland, Oregon, between far-left and far-right extremist groups.

What is different between the two stories above and the examples in the preceding paragraph? The answer is remarkably simple: humanization versus dehumanization, acknowledging people as individuals versus group villainization.

The problem is that in debating or discussing different viewpoints, we are all too quick to categorize and group those with opposing viewpoints as inferior to us, to ascribe to them negative (or sometimes nonhuman) characteristics, and to declare them the enemy.

That is wrong. Simply wrong.

Just as we should hope that no one will so categorize, group, and condemn us, we should not do it to anyone else.

How do we prevent this? One way is to have a face-to-face dialogue with those with whom we disagree—a dialogue in which we seek to understand rather than to be understood, where we try to find solutions to common issues or at least understand more about different viewpoints.

A very recent and important example of this is a project called America in One Room, coordinated by the Center for Deliberative Democracy at Stanford University. It brought together a representative sample of 526 politically and demographically diverse Americans to discuss some of today's most controversial issues and broke the participants into smaller groups of thirteen to fifteen people. The result: more civility in discussions, more focus on the facts, and more potential grounds for solutions.[148]

Based on a recent study, 75 percent of us believe that we should work together to find common ground.[149] That 75 percent includes the vast majority of the so-called silent generation (those currently age seventy-four to ninety-one), baby boomers (those currently age fifty-five to seventy-three), and moderates.

You might ask, as I did, who is in the 25 percent that believe you must stand up for your point of view and never compromise? The largest demographics in that category were millennials (those currently age twenty-three to thirty-eight) and those with a high trust in Washington. This group was also the most likely to have stopped talking with friends and family about policy issues, left a business or company because of political beliefs, and lost friends because of political differences.[150]

Translated to what we expect from our political leaders, the data was relatively similar. Seventy-nine percent of respondents believe that our political leaders must demonstrate civility, authenticity, and respect, while 21 percent believe that our political leaders must fight for what is right, even if that means getting aggressive and rude with the opposition.[151]

Nearly 70 percent saw a role for our nation's colleges and universities to help increase political civility in our country.[152] This is compelling and somewhat surprising data. What is compelling is that a clear majority of us see a role for educational institutions, and especially America's colleges and universities, to help improve political civility. What is somewhat surprising is that colleges and universities have appeared to do exactly the opposite by shielding students from opposing viewpoints.

Regardless of whether these survey results are perception or reality, it demonstrates an opportunity: an opportunity for colleges and universities to take a leading role in helping improve political civility. Such a role is aligned with most, if not virtually all, colleges' and universities' missions.

We the People cannot leave the responsibility for improving civility to colleges and universities. We need to accept responsibility for this important effort as well.

How can we do this? The same way we try to resolve other issues on which there is strong disagreement: consideration and compassion. Before you reject this seemingly "touchy-feely" approach, I'd ask you to think about a strong disagreement you've had with a spouse, a child, a coworker, a friend. What was more effective at resolving the disagreement: Continuing to argue your point until the other side got it? Boycotting them or trying to demean them or their position? Or was it like with Ms. Atwater and Mr. Ellis, starting to listen to the other person or position, to consider the issue from the other person's perspective and to show human concern for them?

We all know which was more effective, don't we?

Instead of doing the first two, let's commit to do the last, both individually and as part of groups to which we belong. When there is an opposing viewpoint, let's:

- Allow the other person/side to express their position and not prevent them from speaking.
- Approach what they say by seeking to understand their position and why they have that position, rather than immediately thinking why it is wrong and our debate points to respond to it.
- Try to find common ground or common principles on which we can begin to have a discussion, rather than look for ways that the other person or position is wrong and evil.
- Try to understand the proponent of the opposite position as human and to treat them with compassion, rather than dehumanizing them and making them the enemy.
- Try kindness and understanding rather than rudeness or aggression.

Let's treat each other, and especially those advocating for viewpoints different than our own, as fellow humans and citizens and as our neighbors.

CHAPTER 15

COURAGE AND COMMITMENT TO GET THE FACTS

Just as the vast majority of Americans believe that there is more negativity and less respect in political debate in the United States, a vast majority of Americans also believe that political debates are not fact based.[153]

This is indeed troubling. If We the People cannot ensure that political debates in our country are based on facts, how can we possibly address not only the civility of those debates but also solve many of the pressing problems that we face today?

The problem appears to be that we don't sufficiently challenge each other, especially those with whom we agree, to use facts in these debates and discussions. We tolerate statements that are not fact based—sometimes even deliberate lies—if we believe the position that these "nonfacts" are used to support. We not only tolerate this failure to support arguments with facts, but those involved in these debates, whether directly or reporting them such as the media, also fail to require fact-based support for these positions and rarely call out made-up facts, no facts, or lies.

Increasingly, we (and, in particular, our current President, Donald Trump) use nonfact statements such as "people say" or "people tell me" to provide factual support, when—regardless if any people have so spoken—there is nothing to support what these unnamed "people" have said, only that they may have said it.

These pseudo-facts are used so pervasively that we have diminished our ability to discern the actual facts and data. Worse, when actual facts and data are used, we have allowed those in the debate to disarm their use by labeling them "false news," saying—without any factual support—that they are not true or attacking the person coming forward with the facts as biased or evil.

Similarly, because of a point-of-view mass media (as discussed previously), we do not have a reliable source to fact-check statements made by government leaders, government agencies, candidates, and others who are part of our governmental and political processes.

The result: we don't have confidence in being able to get the truth in the increasing volume of information with which we are confronted every day. Because we don't know what to believe, we've stopped any meaningful quest for the truth and just default to believing what feels right to us or is consistent with our viewpoints.

Without real facts, is it any wonder that we have become so divisive and uncivil in our political discourse? We have become so divisive because the spin we receive is polarized and extreme. We have become so uncivil because the spin masters believe that the best way to drown out any remaining kernels of truth is to attack the truth tellers and repeat at a higher volume and verbal intensity the lies and the spin the extremes wish us to believe.

Why can't we get to the truth?

There are a number of reasons, but let me highlight a few.

First, we do not have readily available, reliable, unbiased, independent truth discerners. With few exceptions, the information sources we consume today are biased point-of-view spinners, not truth finders. Two principal reasons for this result are economics and technology.

The economic model to support mass media communications shifted from a predominant subscription-based model to a predominantly advertising-based model. And the advertising-based model was no longer based on the size of the ad but on the number of views or clicks the ads generated. As "news" became readily available without a subscription on the internet, revenues from subscriptions for traditional print media declined. As subscriptions declined, the number of readers did, which decreased the value of the advertisements, thus reducing advertising revenue. In contrast, the internet "news" revenue model was (and is) one that relies predominantly on advertising, and rather than being a fixed-price model, it was (and is) a dynamic revenue model based on the number of views or clicks. Thus, the pressure became how to generate views (eyeballs) and clicks. Boring, just-the-facts news doesn't generate a lot of eyeballs and clicks, especially when we focus now so much more on the headlines and conclusions than on longer, investigative analysis. We just don't have time nor wish to make the time for reading more than a few lines. Therefore, those few lines have to be eye- and click-catching to generate revenue.

The technology also changed, as described above, to instant, online, and social—components that did not exist in traditional print media. Instant meant you could get the "news" immediately, which appealed to our desire to be the first to know. Instant also meant that "news" was pushed out without the controls that ensured such "news" met basic journalistic (and truth) standards. Given the choice to get it right or get it out, we chose to get it out because if it didn't get out there, it would miss the views and clicks that generated revenues.

Online meant that even the most geographically isolated or niche publishers could compete for revenues as easily as established, traditional publishers. Online removed virtually any barriers to entry and made scale and scope irrelevant. Indeed, online meant not only that organizations could be publishers but that individuals could be, too, and that with the right "spin," they could make a lot of money. With so many publishers with varying (or no) journalistic standards, we have been (and are) flooded with so much information that purports to be—but is not—factual, with little ability to distinguish between facts and spin. Importantly, as a result, even traditional publishers abandoned journalistic standards to help us discern facts from spin, as they were forced to compete with online publishers.

Social meant that we saw "news" socially—that is, we wanted the news aligned with the groups to which we belonged or desired to belong. We followed (and liked) the news our social networks (existing or desired) followed, regardless of whether we believed that "news" was factual or not. Indeed, this is exactly what some social media sites do. Using algorithms and monitoring individual's usage on their sites, they deliver "news" aligned to those individuals' preexisting views. Social media publishers no doubt realized that selective news delivery met our primitive needs to be social and aligned with other human beings. As a result, the largest "publisher" of news was no longer a traditional media outlet but a social networking site—Facebook.[154]

The combination of instant, online, and social also meant instantaneous, anonymous comments. As discussed above, these have unfortunately further distanced us from discerning the truth as these comments have limited (or where they exist, ineffective) checks on content and validity of source. There is some evidence that these comments have been subject to foreign misinformation campaigns.[155] They are often mean-spirited, divisive, polarizing, biased, and dehumanizing—everything we learned that worsens, not improves, political discourse. This is in contrast to both content and source validity checks that applied to traditional print media news sources.

Some of you might say, well, aren't there laws to handle people saying false things? Isn't that libel or slander? You would think that's true, but our current libel and slander laws can't effectively deal with this situation.

First, in the United States, a public official can't sue for libel or slander just because someone said something untrue or even knowingly false about or involving that official. Public officials are very loosely defined, so it means just about anyone associated with government, including the president, elected officials, and many government employees and even those who publicly advocate to the government. To sue them, you have to not only prove that the statement was false but also that it was made with actual malice. That's a very tough standard, one that has rarely been met.[156]

Moreover, some government officials have absolute immunity from suit while conducting government business, such as congressional representatives' statements in Congress or judges' statements in their decisions or in court. And the president? He or she has virtually absolute immunity from libel laws: he or she can lie—even when he or she knows a statement to be false—without any legal consequence.

For all these reasons, when I hear people say that if the statement about or made by a government official weren't true, why doesn't someone sue (and if no one does, the statement must be true), this is the reason. Flipped around, if you know you can't be sued for saying something false about a public official, or if you're a public official, you can't be sued for saying something false, doesn't that incentivize you to do so?

Second, as with any lawsuit, you have to prove not just liability (a false statement and, if a public official, actual malice), you also have to prove damages. That's also tough. You have to show some monetary or other direct loss. You could perhaps get an injunction (an order not to keep repeating a false statement) if you proved liability, but it costs a lot to bring a lawsuit (and in the United States, the winner of a lawsuit isn't generally entitled to reimbursement of legal fees), so if there aren't any damages, who but perhaps the ultra-wealthy are even going to bother suing?

Third, with regard to anonymous comments, the largest publishers, such as Facebook, aggressively resist all attempts to disclose the identity of those publishing comments on their sites.[157] Even if you wanted to sue and had a case and the money to prosecute it, you'd need to know the person or entity who made the comments to be able to sue.

What, you might ask, can be done about this situation? We can't change economics and technology, and we don't want to have endless libel lawsuits between politicians—how will that solve anything?

The answers actually might be simpler than that, even though there would be—and very recently—have been vehement objections to the solutions that make the most sense.

First, we should treat all publishers equally—both traditional print media publishers and online media (including social media) publishers. We know how to do this—we've done it before. All publishers regardless of medium should be held to journalistic standards to ensure adequate vetting of information they publish as to both content and source. All publishers should be liable for publishing false statements that they have not verified.

Why are we not doing this? It goes back to something we identified as we started this journey: money and influence. Today's large publishers, such as Facebook, not only don't want to recognize that they are publishers and don't want to take any responsibility that they should undertake in that role, but in some cases they want to affirmatively use the rights of publishers to censor information on their sites.[158] They use First Amendment arguments to say they can't or shouldn't censor information. But if that argument were true, then century-old libel laws would all be unconstitutional, and they're not.[159] It would cost money to assume the responsibilities of publishers—a cost these multibillion-dollar companies don't want to undertake. It might also cost revenues, since a more factual-based or delayed (to allow fact-checking) news publication may reduce or delay clicks or views, which is a key basis for their revenue streams. These publishers want the benefit of these revenue streams without undertaking the corresponding burdens or costs that traditional publishers used to undertake to provide us, We the People, with more factual and reliable information. These publishers have been forced to admit that their "publications" have been manipulated and have manipulated our political processes—yet they steadfastly refused to take the appropriate responsibility to prevent this manipulation.[160]

Second, we have allowed, perhaps incrementally, our political leaders, including our president, to recite false information and untruths with little effective challenge. We must force these leaders to provide support for their statements and not allow them to inject knowing lies and unsupportable spin into the political debate in order to manipulate and deceive us from seeing the truth, the actual facts. All media sources need to more effectively use old-fashioned journalistic tools, combined with new information technologies, to fulfill their duty to help us to discern truth from lies, facts from spin. For example, the media need to call out our political leaders on statements that lack factual support, regardless of whether that media source agrees with that statement or not. This can so much more easily be done since we virtually all hold in our hands a tool—that is, the smartphone—that can be used to get the source documents, prior statements of that public official, as well as verifiable data sources, that can be used in real time to call out untruths and spin with actual, provable facts. This can be a way for these media sources to regain the credibility they have lost. We have allowed the media—on all sides of issues and political viewpoints—to promulgate false and misleading statements that are rarely corrected, or if they are, with substantially less visibility than the misleading statement.

Third, we need to be more savvy at detecting lies and spin and more courageous to call them out, including and especially to our social networks. We must commit to take the time to learn the truth, not just gloss over provocative headlines or get our news from tweets but to find credible news sources and even look at source documents. This is where schools, colleges, and universities can play a part to include as part of mandatory civics or other similar curricula, education on helping us be better assessors of truth in the current information age. We also need to seek out alternative viewpoints and more fact-based sources of our information, rather than those sources that are most visible and attention grabbing. The current trend to justify not reading anything more than a tweet, TL; DR (too long, didn't read), is a lame excuse.[161] For sure, news media can and should do a better job of simplifying and condensing information while maintaining journalistic standards. However, this is our duty as citizens, and we must all accept this responsibility as part of the vast benefits we receive as citizens and residents of this country.

CHAPTER 16

CURIOSITY

"When something is confrontational, be curious." That's some of the best advice I've ever received for successfully navigating controversial issues or topics. Yet, our most frequent response to confrontation is more confrontation. As in life, as in politics: such an approach rarely leads to a productive resolution (or any resolution) of the underlying issue or issues.

Here's how we can reframe the debate, with a simple question, a question we all learned how to ask when we were very young: why? Why is a great way to get to the bottom of an issue, to understand the key drivers, and to find a solution. Indeed, it is such a good way to do it that the concept of Five Whys is a tool used to find the root cause of a product or safety failure or other similar problems. The thesis of this tool is that asking why at least five times in reviewing the stated cause of an incident helps get to the root cause. For example, assume that the issue we are trying to solve is reduced state tax revenues. The Five Whys might go something like this:

1. Why are tax revenues decreasing? Answer: Business income taxes are decreasing significantly.

2. Why are business income taxes decreasing significantly? Answer: Businesses are moving their headquarters to other locations.
3. Why are businesses moving their headquarters to other locations? Answer: Our corporate tax rate is higher than in other locations.
4. Why is our corporate tax rate higher than in other locations? Answer: Politically, we needed to show that corporations were paying a higher tax rate.
5. Why did we need to show that corporations were paying a higher tax rate? Answer: Maybe we didn't need to do that. Perhaps we should have focused on increasing the total amount of business tax revenue and not on the rate since the real goal was to keep individual tax rates the same or lower.

Other tools such as avoiding absolutism (never/always, etc.) are also helpful. For example, if someone uses absolutism, explore the basis for that statement, including examples or situations in which it may not be true.

Our role in dealing with confrontational issues is not to be advocates but to be explorers. Explore the basis for each position using tools like the Five Whys. Explore the facts that are relevant to the issue, including exploring their validity, source, and relevance. Explore different possibilities for resolving the issue than the ones that have been proposed.

This is not always easy, but try it. You'll see how mutual exploration is so much more effective than yelling at each other for solving issues.

We'll put this to the test in the next section in which we will use the tools we've discussed in this section as we explore some of the most divisive but important issues we face today.

To summarize:

OUR FRAMEWORK

- Define mutual purpose.
- Gather relevant facts and information.
- Consider alternative solutions.

DOS	DON'TS
Take accountability and responsibility	Make up your own facts
Fix the problem	Believe your facts are superior
Have compassion and caring	Use absolutes or polarize into "sides"
Work with courage and commitment	Create victim-villain stories
Be curious	Allow dehumanizing words or actions

PART IV

EXAMPLES AND POTENTIAL SOLUTIONS

INTRODUCTION

In this final part, we'll explore some of the most controversial issues we face as a nation today. These issues were chosen not just because they are controversial and important, but also because they demonstrate some of the traps, some of the don'ts we have fallen into in addressing and debating these issues. By understanding a potential framework for discussing these issues constructively, the hope is that We the People can find a set of potential solutions.

Again, note that these are *potential* solutions and that the proposed framework is one that we can use to get *unstuck* on many of these issues. The goal is to reset the framework and explore potential paths to a solution so that we and our elected and appointed officials, policy advocates, and the media can help forge solutions or even partial solutions to address these issues.

I believe that one of the causes of political divisions in our country is that some of us have felt that we have not had a voice in discussing these issues. Each of us, regardless of the differences in our viewpoints, has the right to be heard in a respectful, constructive conversation on these issues. Too often and especially recently, we have stifled those voices in the name of "political correctness" or ensuring "emotional safety" and often have denigrated those who are trying to have a voice through name-calling ("deplorables," "elitists," "Never Trumpers," etc.). CNN recently interviewed ten Pennsylvania voters, and what was striking is that one of those voters was talked over (as were others). She then said, "And the way I'm being treated right now is a perfect example of why I will vote for Donald Trump because my voice matters and I won't be talked over."[162]

We have "talked over" viewpoints with which we disagree for too long. Doing so has been a significant part of the political (and other) divisions in our country. When people feel they do not have a voice, they feel marginalized and minimized, and they begin to develop negative emotional feelings. When they finally feel that they have a voice, that voice may become tainted by those negative, emotional feelings, and then that previously suppressed voice can become offensive and, sometimes, abusive.

There is a middle ground: allowing, even encouraging, everyone to have a voice—a respectful voice—without fear for having spoken and without being personally attacked, minimalized, or marginalized. We also need to speak out against abusive voices, name-calling, and gaslighting, especially when this is done by those who share our political views.

We the People need to forge a better path: a path of listening to viewpoints, especially those with which we disagree, a path of not disparaging others because of their viewpoints, a path of seeking to understand rather than to be understood, a path of making all of us belong, rather than being marginalized or minimized. As former Presidential Candidate Pete Buttigieg recently said, "The American experience is defined not by exclusion but by belonging."[163]

Let us find a way for all of us to belong, for all of us to have a voice as we work together to solve the many significant issues we face today.

To do this, I ask that as we begin this exploration that we put aside, as best we can, any emotions involving these issues and that we remain curious and, perhaps most importantly, that we listen. Let's begin.

CHAPTER 17

THE WRONG LABELING DISTRACTS FROM THE REAL ISSUE: CLIMATE CHANGE

What we have called "climate change" is one of the most important and divisive issues we face not only as a nation but as humans. It is an example where we've used labels, here "climate change," as shorthand to identify a group of issues that we haven't clearly defined. On this issue, let's ditch the label "climate change" and discuss the underlying issue without a label, starting with mutual purpose.

Here is what I think that mutual purpose is: we would like clean air, clean water, and a clean environment for ourselves, our children, our grandchildren, and their grandchildren. Or perhaps stated conversely, we don't want polluted air, polluted water, and a polluted environment. No reasonable person (despite political beliefs, socioeconomic status, geography, race, etc.) is for pollution, right?

If we all agree that we want a clean, and not a polluted, environment, then let's identify the facts that we'll need that are relevant to this issue. Here are some of them:

- What are current levels of air, water, and ground pollution?
- What levels of air, water, or ground pollution would be considered safe or clean?
- What is the current difference between the current levels and safe or clean levels?
- Why does the current level of pollutants exceed a safe or clean level? Are there specific pollutants that are causing this more than others? What is the root cause? Is it our policies? Economics? Global competitiveness?

There are probably other facts and other questions to get at additional facts that are important to this issue, but let's stop here for now.

Note that we didn't define the issue by perceived *consequences* of the issue, such as, is the temperature of the earth warmer or not—that is, do we have "global warming?" We also didn't explore, because it wasn't necessary, another consequence that has framed the debate, whether there is climate change, and the cause of that change or whether that change is good or bad. We didn't need to go down any of those divisive rabbit holes since we identified a mutual purpose on which the vast majority of us would agree— clean air, water, and the environment. Rather than jumping to a consequence or, even worse, a solution, we identified a set of facts that are important to the real issue: pollution.

Let's go further. Let's identify how we would go about getting the relevant facts in an unbiased manner. Since we've defined the issue as pollution, we can identify specific pollutants (at least the most significant ones) and find out about them. What levels of those pollutants exist in various places, and what is a "safe" level? The former is what we've called a verifiable fact: the level of a pollutant is x. No judgment needed, just a standard and unbiased measurement, most of which probably already exists. The latter is what we'll call a standard, which is based on experts' opinions based on data and science. There is probably little disagreement about this, especially as to pollutants that have been extensively researched. If there is disagreement, let's carefully examine the facts to see where there is agreement and explore potential biases (e.g., supporting a predetermined outcome, supporting an individual economic interest, supporting a predetermined political outcome, etc.) in outlying data.

Notice, too, that we've kept the facts relevant to a cause, not an effect. We want to measure the cause—pollution—not an effect, such as "warming" or "change," which are not directly relevant to the issue we've identified and may not help with a solution. For example, whether the earth is warmer or colder may be a symptom (or not) of pollution, but there could be other facts leading to "warmer" or "colder" temperatures that are unrelated to not having clean air or water. Pollution, what we've identified is our issue, is either there or not at levels that are—within a defined range—safe or not.

The next step is exploring why we have pollutants that are above a safe level. This requires even more work and fact gathering, including identifying the source of the pollutants, what happens after they are created or released, and then why current solutions haven't been effective in keeping the levels within safe limits. This is where some may start to affix blame—for example, it's those government policies, or those greedy corporations, or the like. But let's avoid such blame, at least until and unless we have facts to support it. Similarly, let's not avoid identifying something as a cause because it might lead some of us to feel that we will be blamed. Let's focus on identifying the cause with the goal of fixing the problem.

With all that work done, we can then focus on potential solutions. Again, as we think about those solutions, let's recognize a few things: there are few, if any, either/or solutions and that existing proposed solutions are not the only ones available to us. For each potential solution, there are relevant pros and cons: advantages and disadvantages to that solution. We'll need to identify those. Again, to the extent we can do this by listening to the competing interests, all the better.

For example, let's say we've identified Pollutant A as the cause of 30 percent of pollution levels above a safe level. One solution would cost $100 billion and would result in a 1 percent increase in unemployment but would be implementable in three years, with a 99 percent chance of reducing the level of Pollutant A to a safe level. Another solution would cost $10 billion and would not result in a significant unemployment change but would take ten years to implement, with an 85 percent chance of reducing the level of Pollutant A to a safe level. There are probably many, many other solutions we could identify. We could do part of one solution and parts of others and get to an optimal solution, or just by identifying a range of potential solutions, we might discover another solution we hadn't previously thought of.

Let's avoid one other thing that we're tempted to do in this type of debate: asking, "Who is going to pay for this?" That question is usually asked to cut off potential solutions. For sure, we should consider as a pro or a con the economic effects of a potential solution—just as we do in our own personal lives—but let's hear all the options first and then we can brainstorm potential solutions to any "Who's going to pay for this?" concerns. We, as a nation, are so fortunate to have so many different ways of deploying resources that there is likely an appropriate, principled-based solution to resolve cost issues. We may, for example, pick the $10 billion solution over the $100 billion one, but that doesn't mean we should not pick *any* solution because we use cost as a "can't."

Notice, again, this is not how we have framed this debate in our country or globally. We often start with the solution or a politically framed label for a solution—for example, a Green New Deal—without having done the work to define the issue, examine its cause, and explore potential solutions. Sometimes we have even name-called or otherwise mocked proponents or opponents of a solution by labeling them socialists, greedy, or providing examples of freezing temperatures in one location to say there is no issue because there is no "global warming." Again, none of this has been, or will ever be, helpful in resolving this issue.

One other issue involving global pollution involves global competitiveness. Specifically, the issue is whether the United States would put itself at an economic disadvantage by incurring expenses to reduce pollution when it is competing against countries that decline to incur those expenses and continue to and increase their pollution. Since pollution is a global issue and to ensure there is fair competition, there are a number of potential solutions. Those solutions could include: (1) a "pollution tariff" that would apply to goods produced in countries that do not reduce their pollution; (2) a "pollution recovery charge" on domestic sellers of products imported from countries that do not reduce their pollution, and/or; (3) labeling or other regulatory requirements that would identify products that come from countries that do not reduce their pollution.[164] There are already parallels for each of these.[165]

We the People need to insist that our elected and appointed officials correctly define "climate change/global warming" as the issue it really is—pollution—and that we get actual, scientific, unbiased data about the real issue, pollution, not its potential effects. Then, using that data, we can identify alternative solutions to factually identify issues that we can debate on the merits, make decisions about, and then implement quickly and efficiently. As we do this, we need to stay focused on our mutual purpose (clean air, water, and environment) and facts (not effects, conclusions, or irrelevant issues) to arrive at an optimal set of solutions that are likely not to please any "side" but that will deliver real results for us, We the People.

CHAPTER 18

MIXING UP RELIGION WITH CIVIL LAW: SAME-SEX "MARRIAGE"

Another controversial example of using wrong labels is "marriage." Although the issue of same-sex "marriage" has largely been resolved in most countries, it really shouldn't have been as controversial as it was. The reason it was: we violated our own Constitution by not separating "church" and "state," religious terms from civil law terms.[166] Getting our terminology right—constitutionally right—at the outset would have gotten us to a long-term solution more quickly and with less collateral damage. The problem is that on this issue and others, we use terms associated with our personal beliefs (which we are allowed to have under the Constitution) but attempt to impose those beliefs—through those terms—on others (which we are not allowed to do under the Constitution). Therefore, after debriefing the "gay marriage" issue, we'll turn to a related issue: religious freedom.

The specific term "marriage" originated sometime between 900 and 1300 AD. It had a religious context, primarily from the Roman Catholic Church, as being a monogamous relationship between a man and a woman as "husband" and "wife." The church prescribed certain rules for "marriages," including but not limited to a very limited ability to end a marriage, called divorce. As part of the U.S. debate on who can "marry," its religious origins have been used in an attempt to define it. Specifically, those who opposed same-sex marriage, and regrettably mixed-race marriage earlier in our history, often cited religious reasons for that opposition.

What has been remarkable about the debate of same-sex marriage is that we've mixed religious and civil concepts, resulting in a blending of terms that has not been helpful or, in fact, consistent with our Constitution. Instead of this mixing, we should have recognized, based on our heritage of religious freedom, that there is a state-recognized "union" of two individuals, let's call it a "civil union," and a religious "union" of two individuals, called a "marriage" or otherwise as defined by that religion, as to which the government—under the principle of separation of church and state—should have no involvement.

If we had approached the issue in that way—that is, a state-recognized-and-defined union of two individuals separate from a religious definition of that union—perhaps we could have come to a better or less acrimonious solution to the issue of same-sex (and before that, mixed-race) "marriages." Specifically, to achieve the *civil* rights, benefits, and obligations of a civil union, individuals would have to follow the *civil* rules of such unions, as defined by the government. The government could, as it does, prohibit nonconsensual unions, unions involving children under an age of consent, or unions with other species or inanimate objects. It could encourage such unions by providing governmental benefits such as lower tax rates or financial support for families—all of which would be completely separate from religious considerations.

For sure, governments could have avoided the controversy

caused by mixing civil and religious terminology, such as "marriage licenses" and tax statuses such as "married filing jointly." However, we did not, and this mixing, in my opinion, caused the issue of same-sex marriages to be more complicated and divisive than it needed to be. We could have accommodated religious beliefs by allowing—as we must under the Constitution—religions to define who they would or would not recognize as part of a "marriage" or similar religious term; and we could have accommodated those without religious beliefs or those who wished to have a union without prescribing to religious requirements by having civil unions. Since the governmentally recognized rights, benefits, and responsibilities of civil unions would apply equally to everyone, we would also have met constitutional rights of equal protection under the laws.

Where we got off track is allowing those with firmly held religious beliefs to attempt to impose their religious beliefs on others, using a term with religious origins to describe a nonreligious status and failing to focus on the real constitutional issues: separation of church and state and equal protection.

The other side to this and similar debates is the right to religious freedom. That debate takes many forms: public prayers, displays of religious symbols, and even more recently homework assignments involving the study of different religious beliefs. For now, and with the interest of keeping this brief (avoiding TL; DR) and related to same-sex unions.

Again, it's important that we are very careful with our terms, the language of our Constitution, and we approach this with common sense. Let's start with some principles that, hopefully, most of us can agree with:

1. Under the Constitution, each American has the right to choose their own religion or to not choose any religion at all.
2. We are free to practice our chosen religion, or not to practice a religion, as long as we don't physically harm another person (e.g., flogging or sacrificing others) or interfere with their rights to practice a religion or none at all.
3. We cannot be treated differently by government, or governmental actors, because of our chosen religion or our choice not to have a religion.

Let's add one more thing: like all rights, sometimes certain rights may conflict with other rights. In those instances, we should find a solution that optimizes the exercise of all rights equitably.

One final thing as we work together to find a solution consistent with the principles above, let's focus just on resolving that specific issue, what I'll call the main event, and not get distracted by other issues, what I'll call sideshows.

Let's use wedding cakes as an example. This is a real issue, one that went all the way to the U.S. Supreme Court—twice. The issue is whether a baker (and the bakery he or she owns) who holds religious beliefs that do not support same-sex marriage can be compelled to bake a "wedding" cake for a same-sex couple. Before we get going on the emotions, let's look at this issue based on our agreed principles above. To do that, let's say that the cake isn't a "wedding" cake; it's just a cake or a pie ordered not in conjunction with a "wedding."

Can the baker and bakery refuse to sell a cake or pie to a same-sex couple? Can the baker and bakery refuse to allow a same-sex couple to eat the cake or pie in the bakery? I think we would all agree that the answer to both questions is no. Why? Because selling a cake or allowing it to be eaten in a place open to the public doesn't affect the baker's right to religious beliefs and also respects a same-sex couple's rights to equal treatment as long as the baker and bakery would sell the cake or pie to different-sex couples or individuals.

Another example: Let's say a same-sex couple goes to a bakery on a religious campus—for example, a seminary—and wants to order communion wafers. I think all of us would agree that the seminary can certainly decline to sell them communion wafers, which the seminary and church believe have religious meaning. This respects the seminary's religious belief that only those who follow that religion's beliefs can partake of certain objects identified with those religious beliefs.

Now let's tackle the issue of the "wedding" cake. How can we respect both the baker's/bakery's right to religious freedom and the same-sex couple's right to equal rights? Let's start first with what about a "cake" could make it religious or interfere with a religious belief. An undecorated cake itself doesn't, right? A cake is a cake. What about the baker's right not to have to support a religion or nonreligion to which he or she does not ascribe? Identifying the bakery as the maker of a decorated cake might imply that the baker supports or endorses same-sex marriage, which is against his or her religious beliefs. What is at least one potential way to accommodate both groups' rights?

Since we agree there is nothing religious about an undecorated cake, the baker could make a generic wedding cake without a topper depicting same-sex couples or a religious belief to which he or she does not ascribe. The same-sex couple could put their own topper or other symbols that may impact religious beliefs on the cake. The same-sex couple could agree not to make any statement that would imply the baker's endorsement of a principle that is against his or her religious belief. The baker could deliver the cake to the building in which a "wedding" reception is held without being perceived as endorsing a religion, noting that he or she likely delivers "wedding" cakes to receptions of heterosexual couples with different religious beliefs other than his or her own. The baker should not be required to participate in the "wedding" ceremony of the same-sex couple (or any couple for that matter).

Notably, none of these are all-or-nothing solutions tipped in favor of one side or the other—that is, the baker can refuse to make a "wedding" cake without any limitations or the baker must make a "wedding" cake without any limitations.

By avoiding these all-or-nothing solutions, we can respect both religious freedom and equal rights in a way that doesn't divide us.

CHAPTER 19

IMMIGRATION

Now let's return to another divisive issue, broadly defined as "immigration." It's a big issue that has many different components. To help us find a framework to resolve this issue, we'll first break it down into some of those components, look for mutual purpose, examine the facts and data, and consider potential solutions.

One major way to break down the immigration issue is to address current immigrants (i.e., those currently in the United States) from future immigrants (i.e., those who seek to enter the United States). Let's start there.

What could be some mutual purposes as to current immigrants in the United States (in no particular order)?

- Find a way to address current immigrants and resolve their status.
- Appropriately address any security (e.g., crime) issues created by current immigrants.
- Appropriately address any economic (e.g., jobs, governmental support, overall economy) issues created by current immigrants.

- Address current immigrants fairly and consistent with constitutional values.

I think we could all agree that these are consensus mutual purposes, even though we may have different views about how to address those mutual purposes and what the issues underlying those mutual purposes are.

What are the relevant facts related to current immigrants?

- Number of current undocumented immigrants in the United States.
- Number of current undocumented immigrants in the United States who financially support themselves and their families.
- Number of American citizens' jobs displaced by undocumented immigrants.
- Crime statistics involving undocumented immigrants (including comparison to citizens).
- Government support provided to undocumented immigrants (type and cost). This would also include any educational or other preferences to undocumented immigrants.
- Current regulations/immigrant control (including entry points of undocumented immigrants, enforcement of immigration control, current immigration policies).

I think we would all agree, again without getting into our individual or collective positions on undocumented immigration, that these are important facts that should inform the debate of this issue. How do we get this data and ensure its validity? Some partisans have, wrongly and politically, framed this need for data collection around asking a citizenship question in the 2020 census. But that is the wrong issue. A question on the census about whether someone is or is not a citizen will not provide the information, described above, that we need. Let's call the census citizenship question for what it is: a political sideshow. One side of the issue wants the citizenship question because it may suppress noncitizens from responding to the census because they fear their answer will lead to their deportation and, as a result, reduce electoral votes and/or federal funding in states where there are more undocumented immigrants. The other side of the issue doesn't want the citizenship question because they want to include undocumented immigrants to increase or maintain electoral votes and federal funding in states where there are more undocumented immigrants. Let's not take the bait that both sides are dangling in front of us on this issue. Let's focus on the main event and not the sideshow.

There are already many, many existing sources of this data that we can use to inform our discussion and that can lead us to a range of potential solutions. Let's get that data and information.

With that data, there are probably a range of solutions that could include:

- Devoting resources to make individual determinations on each undocumented immigrant's status that would include a criminal background check, payment of any unpaid taxes, and ensuring that we do not put documented family members on government support rolls as a result of deporting the undocumented immigrant that financially supports those family members.
- Agreeing that undocumented immigrants who fail (standard to be determined) a criminal background check are deported.
- Understanding (with data) any displacement of citizen workers as a result of undocumented immigrants and providing support to those workers to regain jobs.

- Understanding (with data) any preferences given to undocumented immigrants or immigrants that become citizens or legal residents and examining such preferences to ensure that undocumented immigrants or those who become citizens or legal residents do not receive greater preferences than citizens or other citizens.

Next let's turn to future immigration.

Most of us could probably agree on the following mutual purposes:

- We should develop immigration policies that do not return us to a situation where undocumented immigrants are allowed to enter the United States.
- We should develop immigration policies that enhance our current and future economic development and global competitiveness.
- We should develop immigration policies that do not diminish our domestic safety and security.
- We should develop immigration policies that minimize economic effects on existing citizens.
- We should develop immigration policies that reflect different types of immigration, including economic immigration, family unity immigration, and humane immigration (e.g., what we currently call asylum-based immigration).

Based on that common purpose, we would probably need the following facts and information, among others:

- Examples of other countries' methods to avoid entry of undocumented immigrants before a determination of their immigration status, including handling and enforcing temporary immigration status designations.

- Determining the number and type of jobs that we will need in the next X years and current gaps, if any, to fill those jobs.
- Current unemployment and underemployment data, including by geography and type of job/skill.
- Current governmental (or other) support or preferences (if any) for immigrants.
- Data about historical immigration (by country of origin, geography, job type, etc.).

Then, from those mutual purposes and with the data above and other similar data, we could develop future immigration policies that are consistent with those mutual purposes and supported by that data.

Notice something about this framework?

We avoided jumping to solutions before we have established mutual purpose and relevant facts. We avoided political positioning and spin. In none of this did we jump to building multibillion-dollar walls, separating undocumented families at the border, providing government-paid healthcare to immigrants, or decommissioning Immigration and Customs Enforcement (ICE). These polarizing extremes haven't helped and won't help us solve these issues, nor has dehumanizing political spin. The immigration issues are solvable if we reject these sideshows and focus, with common purpose, compassion, courage, accountability, and curiosity, with relevant, unbiased data, on the main event.

CHAPTER 20

MISSING THE OBVIOUS BECAUSE OF POLITICAL SQUABBLES: WHY AREN'T WE MORE CONCERNED ABOUT RUSSIA ELECTION INTERFERENCE?

Sometimes we are so caught up in politics that we can't see the real issue right in front of us. Although there are, and have been, many examples of this, one of the most recent is the Mueller Report. That report, as we all know, had two parts: (1) examining whether the Russian government or its operatives interfered in the 2016 presidential election and whether President (then candidate) Trump colluded with such interference; and (2) whether President Trump, after having been elected, obstructed justice by interfering with the investigation of such interference.

What was so frustrating when reading the report,[167] the political spin, and media reporting after its release—many of which provided opinions without having read the report—was that everyone seemed to be missing the issue (and conclusion) that was the most important: that Russia or Russian operatives had in fact interfered in a U.S. presidential election!

Instead, the report became a political football with President Trump falsely claiming the report exonerated him even though it, in fact, specifically said it didn't; with the Democrats calling for more hearings and investigations of Trump's actions; with the attorney general (yes, he's the one who's supposed to represent us) creating a misleading summary and then later, launching a politically motivated counter-investigation into the origin of the Russia investigation.

Instead of us all uniting to work to prevent future interference in our elections, we politically polarized ourselves around unhelpful sideshows. We missed the main event, and we didn't even get the sideshows right.

Here is what the Mueller Report found, without political spin:

- The Russians did in fact interfere in the 2016 presidential election.
- There was insufficient evidence that candidate Trump and his political associates conspired with the Russians regarding that interference.
- That a Russian operative did offer the Trump campaign purportedly damaging information on candidate Clinton, and the highest-level members of the campaign agreed to meet with that operative about that information. Doing so was not a crime.
- There were facts that would support a conclusion that President Trump committed obstruction of justice related to the investigation.

- However, President Trump (or any president) could not be charged with obstruction of justice or other crimes while in office.

We focused on all of these except the first and most important one: the Russians did, in fact, interfere in the 2016 presidential election.

We spent valuable time and effort on the other conclusions, attacking and counterattacking the people involved in the investigation or mentioned in the report, and making all that the main event—even though we all knew that we have another presidential election coming up in 2020.

What should We the People have expected to happen? We should have expected our political leaders, the president and his attorney general, and Congress to have worked together to stop Russian (or any other foreign country) interference in the 2020 presidential election.[168] But that didn't (and almost certainly won't) happen. Instead, we focused on investigating the investigators, investigating the investigation, name-calling, urging foreign governments to investigate 2020 political opponents, editorializing, spinning and speculating about political effects of the report, and using the report for political fundraising purposes.

Rather than uniting us around a common purpose (preventing Russian interference in future elections), these actions further divided us and worsened our political discourse. The political name-calling worsened, we distorted and distracted from the main issue for political purposes, and we started a series of counter-investigations that further distracted from that main issue, preventing any focus on that issue. We used it to stoke emotions on both sides. We lied about what it said and didn't say and repeated those lies to prevent (or fuel the flames) for future spin.

Indeed, one might argue that Russia hit the trifecta of election interference: First, it interfered in those elections in 2016 and escaped any real consequence as a result. Second, the investigation and resulting spin and counter-investigations prevented us from preventing them from interfering in the 2020 election. Third, it increased political polarization and dysfunction in American politics and our elections, making the United States weaker and empowering Russia.

We the People expect our elected officials to work together to identify and solve external threats to our country and its democratic, political processes, including but not limited to election interference. And we expect our elected officials to focus on the real issues, not political sideshows.

CHAPTER 21

HEALTHCARE/MEDICARE: IDENTIFYING THE REAL ISSUES— COSTS, COVERAGE, AND CHOICE

One of the most personal political issues is healthcare. Perhaps more than any other current issue, it has the ability to drive political decision-making. As many have said, this issue may have been the most important cause of the so-called Blue Wave in the 2018 midterm elections. It will also be an important issue in 2020.

For sure, healthcare is a complex issue. In prior elections, and perhaps even today, it's been morphed into a "role of government" issue. This began with the so-called death panels in the 2008 election, where conservatives falsely claimed that government-provided healthcare meant the government would decide who would or would not be provided lifesaving healthcare. More recently, it has been recast as a villain-victim story in which health insurance companies and large healthcare providers are the villains, healthcare consumers are the victims, and the government is the savior by hijacking the popular Medicare program to include coverage for everyone, not just those over sixty-five. There is even a secondary subplot with another villain: wealthy individuals and corporations are cast as villains in the subplot of who will fund Medicare for All.

However, let me suggest that from the perspective of We the People, these issues are not about all that. Rather, it's about the three Cs: costs, coverage, and choice. Let me further suggest that cost and coverage are economic issues and that choice is a highly emotional issue, one that will likely drive decisions on cost and coverage.[169]

With that in mind, let's start with choice.

When it comes to healthcare, choice can mean several things, including the right to choose your doctors, the right to choose a health insurance provider, and the right to choose whether to have health insurance at all. Let me posit that the vast majority of us will demand the right to choose our doctors and the right to choose who provides our health insurance. Some may also want the right to choose not to have health insurance, but that is a right few of us would exercise, so we can call that issue what it is in the larger debate: a sideshow.[170] Also note that the vast majority of employers recognize the importance of choice in healthcare, demonstrated by their offering different options for employee healthcare coverage.

Choice of our health insurance providers has a very practical effect for at least two reasons. These reasons are significant and affect a large number of us, so we should make sure that we identify them. Let's start with Medicare Supplemental Insurance.

As many of us know, Medicare does not cover all healthcare expenses. Sometimes there are significant gaps, beyond just a minimal copay or deductible. As a result, the overwhelming majority of Medicare recipients (90 percent based on data from AARP[171]) have supplemental Medicare health insurance coverage. Although Medicare is provided by the federal government and is paid for by monthly premiums and the Medicare tax assessed to all workers (the overwhelming majority of whom are not current Medicare recipients), supplemental insurance is provided by private (i.e., nongovernmental) health insurers at monthly premiums that vary based on the specific plan that is chosen.

Almost all (94 percent) of Medicare recipients who have supplemental coverage are satisfied with that coverage.[172] Think about that, 94 percent! That is a satisfaction percentage that is rarely achieved even for the most popular and loved consumer products and services. It is significantly higher than overall satisfaction levels for Medicare, which approach 80 percent.[173] And as demonstrated by the many types of available supplemental coverage plans, Medicare supplement consumers like the choice that those plans provide them.

Why hasn't this data—data that somewhat remarkably has not as of this writing—been part of the candidate debates on this issue—informed the "Medicare for All" debate and discussion? (As background, current proposals for "Medicare for All" would provide a single [i.e., only] source of healthcare coverage not only for current Medicare recipients but all Americans. Thus, Medicare supplement insurance could no longer be offered.) That, let me suggest, is politically problematic on several levels. At a basic level, it suggests a lack of understanding of Medicare supplemental insurance and the choice it has provided Medicare recipients. Recipients appear to clearly value the choice of plans and are overwhelmingly satisfied with their chosen coverage. From a different perspective, it raises issues about the role of government for sure, but from a pure political perspective and narrative, the question of who gets to make our healthcare and insurance decisions. To be blunt, it appears to smack of government insiders or academic elites deciding what is best for us, We the People. That is a problem both substantively (we prefer choice) and politically (we don't want political insiders and elites making our decisions for us). Those advocating for Medicare for All or similar no-choice proposals need to carefully consider these proposals in light of our preference for choice (both having a choice and who gets to make the choice).

For many non-Medicare recipients, there is another significant choice issue with a slightly different perspective: employer-funded health insurance plans established and controlled by labor unions. In many labor negotiations, union workers have won, in some cases after a significant fight and giving up on other issues, the right to have their union's health plan, paid for by their employer. This has been an important issue for many unions who have established their own health plans for their members. Let me posit that even though the issue is choice, it is also about control. For these union members, having their health insurance plans controlled by their union, rather than their employer, is very important to them. This choice/control should not be overlooked in the Medicare for All debate. As presidential candidate and former Vice President Joe Biden has suggested, these union members are likely going to resist any governmental mandate that would transfer control over their healthcare plans from their unions to the government.

Even non-Medicare recipients and non-union employees attach value to choice in healthcare and other matters. As government skepticism increases, having the federal government make decisions about their healthcare, especially when those choices may be viewed as being made by detached government insiders and political elites who may have ulterior motives, is politically risky and untenable.

We the People want choice in our healthcare coverage.

Now to the other Cs: cost and coverage. Since they are directly related, we'll discuss them together.

Let's start with something that should be obvious but still generates political spin/uncertainty: coverage for preexisting conditions. Although many (or perhaps even most) candidates and elected officials of both parties have announced support for such coverage, their actions are not always aligned with their statements. For example, recent attempts to repeal Obamacare would have repealed preexisting condition coverage, as highlighted in various Democratic Party campaign ads in 2018. Yet, the overwhelming majority of us[174] support such coverage. Why is this still an issue? If it's not an issue, why can't we have clear, bipartisan support and quick passage and enactment of federal legislation that guarantees coverage for preexisting conditions?

Now to the other cost and coverage issues. We've heard from some candidates that under Medicare for All proposals, most of us will pay less or nothing for healthcare and that everything will be covered. Really? The problem is that although such a plan, if it were possible and feasible, would fulfill our wildest dreams and hopes. Coming back to reality, we know that it is not possible and feasible. Even if it were financially possible and feasible, we know that it would create the incentive to seek medical care even when not medically needed and, given the finite number of medical care professionals, might unreasonably delay or deny care to those who need it.

We the People don't expect free or unlimited. We expect affordable cost with appropriate incentives to seek care when needed and to have that care available on a timely basis when it is needed.

These proposals are also infeasible for another reason: they are typically (as in Senator Elizabeth Warren's plan, for example) based on a villain-victim story. Wealthy people (i.e., billionaires) and corporations are going to pay for it because they're evil. People and companies are less supportive of a proposal, especially one that they have to fund, if it requires them to be made the villains. There is no need to do it. As discussed above, creating a funding system that is economically and fact based is all that is needed. Likely, those with more will have to contribute more, but that's a lot more palatable than having to contribute more *and* be villainized for it. Some employers have even adopted similar funding approaches, having a sliding scale of employee contributions that increase by increasing salary bands and/or ensuring that employee contributions do not exceed a certain percentage of employee salaries. These proposals are rarely met with opposition from the higher-contributing employees and are often proposed by such employees.

The final aspect of coverage and cost we'll discuss, again as an example of how to solve these important issues in a way that meets the expectations of We the People and create a bipartisan, commonsense solution, is the issue of reducing healthcare costs and improving outcomes. Shouldn't improving health be the primary goal of healthcare?

One of the best ways to control costs is to provide information about those costs that allow consumers to make a choice based on those costs. Yet in healthcare, there is often little, if any, information about cost prior to the time we receive the bill. We get cost information about almost everything in advance so we can make a decision from among competing providers. Why not for healthcare?

Again, we're back to choice. That same choice should apply with regard to recommended testing and referrals. Most doctors and hospitals provide only a single referral within their own organization. Providing options with costs would allow us to make our own decisions and would surely create more competitive pricing.

Drug pricing is similar. Yes, there is a competing policy argument from manufacturers about the high costs being necessary to encourage research and development. If that is true, then drug manufacturers should bring forward that cost information into the drug pricing and control debate. Again, the point here is to identify the relevant common grounds on which we could agree (keep drug costs low but don't disincentivize drug research and development). Once those common grounds are established, let's bring in the facts (not just spin or policy positions) to inform that debate. Without that, we are at a standstill on any meaningful proposal to solve this issue, including the issue of overprescribing.

Also, to reduce costs, we should encourage and incent wellness and favorable health outcomes. For sure, no one should be stigmatized for health conditions that they cannot reasonably control. However, we each need to be accountable for the cost when we don't take the appropriate actions to try to improve our health. The person who follows the maintenance schedule for their automobile is likely going to avoid many costly repairs. The person who ignores that schedule is likely going to incur many costly repairs. We don't rescue the person who ignores maintenance and subsidize the costly repairs that are the cause of their not taking the appropriate actions. Why should we do that with healthcare?

Again, it's an issue of choice: if I choose to participate in a wellness program and follow what my doctor says, shouldn't I get a break on healthcare costs? Correspondingly, should someone who doesn't participate in a wellness program and doesn't follow what his or her doctor says pay the same as someone who does participate and does follow doctor's orders?

We're not saying the government should (or even could) regulate what we do with our own bodies. That should always be an individual's choice—without a doubt. It's also not about requiring achievement of certain results, which a person can't always control. It's about taking reasonable actions and providing usable tools, in consultation with their chosen healthcare providers who will help improve health, and aligning choice with consequence and benefit with responsibility—as we do for virtually (if not) everything else in our lives.

The path to solving the significant healthcare issues we face are about the three Cs: choice, cost, and coverage, and the most important of these is choice.

CHAPTER 22

GUNS AND INDIVIDUAL RIGHTS AND RESPONSIBILITIES

The gun rights issue is one of the most controversial issues we face today. It is a substantial issue on its own, but to appropriately consider it, we need to deal with the broader issue it involves: individual rights, especially individual rights vis-à-vis the government.

The bedrock for gun rights in the United States is the Second Amendment. Yet, I suspect that most (or perhaps even a substantial majority) of those advocating on either side of the issue have ever read the Second Amendment. That is sad and concerning. Let's start there:

> A well-regulated Militia, being necessary to the security of a free State, the right of the people to keep and bear Arms, shall not be infringed.

First off, do you notice that the first clause, "a well-regulated Militia, being necessary to the security of a free State," is hardly ever identified or discussed in the gun rights debate? Why have we overlooked this important introductory phrase? Here, unlike many other issues we face, we have a clear and contemporaneous identification and agreement on the common purpose on this issue. Let's make sure we understand it.

To do that, let's define the one word in this phrase that we may not all know the meaning of: militia. *Merriam-Webster* defines militia as "a part of the organized armed forces of a country liable to call only in emergency." That's interesting as well.

And note that the militia needs to be "well regulated" and that its purpose is security, and specifically the security of a free state.

Why have we not used these words, clearly part of the Second Amendment, to help us frame the debate regarding the Second Amendment?[175]

This is indeed odd. But it may actually be helpful—putting aside the partisan rhetoric and intense special interest lobbying—to getting us closer to resolving these issues.

It appears that a reading of the entire Second Amendment would reject *both* of the extreme positions that have been taken regarding gun rights:

- That there can be no regulation of guns under the Second Amendment. That is clearly not true, because the purpose of the amendment is clearly stated as a *well-regulated* militia.
- Similarly, that the government can, consistent with the Second Amendment, prohibit gun ownership for all individuals. That is clearly not allowed by the clear text of the amendment, "The right of the people to keep and bear Arms shall not be infringed."

In addition, there is not a right in the Constitution that doesn't have a corresponding responsibility or limits. For example, we have the right to free speech, but we can't shout "Fire!" in a crowded theater or libel or slander someone. Thus, positions that say the right to own and bear arms does not have any corresponding responsibilities are simply wrong—just as ban and seize all gun arguments are equally wrong. Similarly, arguments about the "right to bear arms" being either limited by the type of "arms" that existed in 1789 or conversely that they are unlimited by technology, also miss the mark. As to the latter argument, if it were true—which it is not—citizens would have the right to possess nuclear arms, which all of us would agree is not permitted under the Second Amendment. Instead of trying to win the debate, let's try to solve the issue.

What is the middle ground and common purpose that can form a basis for resolving the issues involving guns in the United States? First, let's start with some facts we would need to address this issue:

- It would be important to understand who currently owns guns in the United States and the reason they use them.[176]
- It would be important to understand the number of deaths caused by guns in the United States by type of death (e.g., murder, suicide, mass shooting) and by shooter (e.g., age and other demographics, mental illness, family member, etc.).
- It would be important to understand what type of regulations apply to U.S. militias (the legal ones), both at the time of the Second Amendment and now, to see if those regulations provide any guidance.
- It would be important to understand what type of regulations and laws apply to similar products or services whose primary purpose is for self-defense or to inflict injury or death (to humans and/or animals). This would include not only pro-phylactic regulation but also after-the-fact liability.

- It would be important to understand what type of regulations and laws apply to products that can be dangerous or cause injury (even if that is not their primary purpose). This would also include not only prophylactic regulation but also after-the-fact liability.

As to common purpose and potential common ground, there already is a lot of common ground. The most recent opinion survey shows there is substantial majority agreement on at least four items:[177]

- Seventy-one percent of us believe we should ban high-capacity ammunition magazines—that is, those containing more than ten rounds.
- Ninety-one percent of us believe that those with mental illness should not be allowed to own guns.
- Eighty-eight percent of us believe that there should be background checks for private gun sales and at gun shows.
- Sixty-nine percent of us believe that assault-style weapons should be banned.

There are likely other items for which there is broad agreement, including banning those on the no-fly list from owning guns.

By examining regulation of similar products (both those whose purpose is to inflict injury or death and other products that can cause such harm or be used in a crime), informed by actual data of gun deaths and injuries, we could start to find a common ground for regulation.

For example, such regulation could include some or all of the following as well as many other creative proposals based on a defined common purpose, consistent with the Constitution:

- That all guns be registered, as is the case for toxic products as well as for automobiles. (And correspondingly, that any non-registered gun is subject to seizure and/or fines and penalties.)

- That all gun owners have and maintain insurance to cover any injuries or deaths caused by their guns, as is required for certain hazardous operations as well as for automobiles. (And correspondingly that any noninsured guns cannot be used.)

- That permits be obtained prior to allowing gun ownership, as is the case for toxic products and automobiles.

- That the registered owner is liable for any use of the gun, as is the case for toxic products and automobiles.

- Gun manufacturers are liable for any illegal use of the gun, just as manufacturers of toxic products are liable for any down-stream use of their products. This could appropriately lead to industry self-regulation of guns to avoid potential liability, just as is the case in other situations, such as toxic products.

- Safety mechanisms to ensure only the owner (or authorized users) uses the gun. This is where technological solutions can really help with this issue. For example, and this is just an idea, I cannot unlock my phone unless my fingerprint is on the small pad or it recognizes my face. Similar technology could prevent unauthorized use of guns as well as documenting for law enforcement who used the gun in any investigation of a crime using the gun.

- Restricting guns from being present in certain locations. Although there is the argument that we need to allow guns to defend against guns in every location, the counter to that argument is that the Second Amendment would not support ubiquitous gun carrying and use, since it is hard to imagine a militia being composed of schoolchildren or needed in a theater, and so forth.

Why haven't we been able to solve these issues, especially when there is such clear majority support of reasonable, constitutionally permissible gun regulation? One answer is the extremes and the special interests each take no-compromise positions. These extremes and special interests thwart the views of us, We the People, overcoming those majority views with money and power. These extremes and special interests inflame each other by taking unreasonable (and unconstitutional) positions like former Congressman Beto O'Rourke's position that the government should seize everyone's guns and the National Rifle Association's position against any regulation of guns because it is a slippery slope leading to gun seizure and blaming the gun problem on mental health.

Another reason is that this issue has been consumed by the broader issue of individual versus government rights—that is, we don't want the government telling us what to do. Fair enough, but that blanket positioning statement isn't helpful toward resolving this issue. If, for example, the policy should be we don't want the government telling us what to do, then taken to its logical extreme, we should have no governmental regulations or laws at all. That, of course, would be anarchy, not the democratic republic established by our Constitution. But why, again, go to the extremes? We don't need to. We can respect individual rights to own guns *and* have reasonable gun regulation based on regulations that apply to other similar products.

We the People have tolerated this thwarting of our will long enough. It's time that our wishes be heard and acted on. Reasonable gun regulation and ensuring appropriate gun ownership is constitutionally permissible and sound policy that the vast majority of us support. We don't have to fix everything at once, but let's fix what we can now, see what effect it has on the problem of gun violence in our country, and then we can decide what, if any, other constitutionally permissible regulations make sense.

CHAPTER 23

ABORTION: INDIVIDUAL RIGHTS AND RELIGIOUS FREEDOM

The abortion issue is perhaps the most divisive issue we have faced as a nation. It encompasses not just the issue itself but a broader examination of the constitutional protections of individual rights and deeply held religious or moral beliefs. It has also been a key component of issues involving the composition of the United States Supreme Court. Virtually every recent Supreme Court confirmation hearing directly involved questioning or trying to ascertain the nominee's position on this issue, becoming a litmus test for whether a nominee will be opposed or supported. It has been used as a vanguard for a host of these issues and others, which has unfortunately obscured the focus on this issue, both as to the facts and the underlying constitutional principles.

As with many other issues, proponents and opponents are often uninformed by the facts and these legal principles, with only a minority having even read the seminal Supreme Court decision *Roe v. Wade*. Instead, they use the decision as a weapon, attributing facts and legal principles to that decision that are inconsistent with it.

This issue is so highly emotional, so personal, so controversial that it has triggered abortion opponents to ironically kill or maim others in an attempt to prevent abortions, as well as violent protests by those who support abortion rights.

As hard as it might be on this issue, let's try to take those strong emotions out of our discussion. To help with this, let us also put to the side legitimate religious beliefs, protected by the Constitution, that without question allow those holding those beliefs to choose not to have an abortion and, without inciting violence or threatening another's rights, to advocate against abortions. I understand that putting those emotions aside may be difficult, but it is important to see whether common ground can be established on this issue.

First, let's start with what *Roe v. Wade* held and didn't hold. For that, let's go to the source: the United States Supreme Court's discussion of *Roe v. Wade* in its subsequent decision, *Planned Parenthood of Pennsylvania v. Casey.*[178] In that decision, the Supreme Court stated that *Roe v. Wade* was based on three principles:

> First is a recognition of the right of the woman to choose to have an abortion before viability and to obtain it without undue interference from the state. Before viability, the state's interests are not strong enough to support a prohibition of abortion or the imposition of a substantial obstacle to the woman's effective right to elect the procedure. Second is a confirmation of the state's power to restrict abortions after fetal viability, if the law contains exceptions for pregnancies which endanger a woman's life or health. And third is the principle that the state has legitimate interests from the outset of the pregnancy in protecting the health of the woman and the life of the fetus that may become a child. These principles do not contradict one another; and we adhere to each.

Let's clear the air about what *Roe v. Wade* held and didn't hold.

- Most basically, it neither held that all abortions are permitted nor that all abortions are prohibited.
- It recognized several important governmental rights, including the right to protect the health of a female carrying a fetus and the government's right to protect a fetus once it is viable outside the womb.
- It also recognized a woman's right to make decisions about her own body, including the right to terminate a pregnancy subject to (or in the case of her own health, consistent with) the government's rights.
- Prior to viability, the woman's right to terminate a pregnancy outweighs the state's right to prevent an abortion.
- After viability, the state has the right to restrict abortions unless continuing the pregnancy endangers the woman's life or health.
- It does not require anyone to have an abortion if they don't want one.
- It does not require anyone to participate in an abortion if they object to it on religious grounds (or any other grounds).

Here is the reason for the dispute in a nutshell: Anti-abortion/pro-life advocates believe that life begins from conception and therefore any abortion is murder, which should be treated as a crime, and that there is not an exception for rape, incest, or the health of the mother, although some pro-life advocates believe in one or more of these exceptions.[179] Pro-abortion/pro-choice advocates believe that the woman's right to an abortion predominates over the rights of the fetus or unborn child, with apparently few exceptions.[180] These virtually "all or nothing" approaches are troubling. For example, a leading pro-life advocacy group's website takes a harsher position on abortion than it does war, assisted suicide, and euthanasia.[181] And a leading pro-choice advocacy group obfuscates on at-birth abortions, skirting the issue by instructing its adherents to state that this involves only 2 percent or fewer of all abortions.[182]

What do most of us believe? Not these positions. As confirmed by recent Gallup polling,[183] only 25 percent of those polled believe that abortion should always be legal and only 21 percent believe that it should always be illegal. This is true even though roughly half of respondents identified themselves as pro-life and the other half (roughly) as pro-choice. Notably, this same, virtually even split of opinion occurred on the question of whether abortion was moral.

Other results:

- The majority (60 percent) believe that we should not overturn *Roe v. Wade.*
- The majority (60 percent) believe that abortions should be legal in the first trimester, whereas only 13 percent believe they should be legal in the third trimester.
- Regarding specific reasons for an abortion:
  ◦ The overwhelming majority (83 percent) believed that abortion should be legal in the first trimester of pregnancy if the mother's life was in danger, with a slightly lower percentage (75 percent) believing it should be legal in the third trimester.
  ◦ The overwhelming majority (77 percent) believed that abortion should be legal in the first trimester in the case of rape and incest, but only 52 percent believed it should be legal in the third trimester.
  ◦ As for a fetal mental disability or Down syndrome, only about half supported legal abortions in the first trimes-

ter (56 percent and 49 percent, respectively), but only a minority supported legal abortions in such cases in the third trimester (35 percent and 29 percent, respectively).

○ Only 45 percent supported abortions for "any reason" in the first trimester, with only 20 percent supporting such abortions in the third trimester.

Although something is not always the right choice just because a majority of people support it, it is notable that the vast majority of Americans not only do not support overturning *Roe v. Wade* but also generally support the principles on which that decision is based.

It is clear that there are divided moral and ethical opinions on the issue of abortion. And as with many such issues that involve personal beliefs, there is nothing wrong with such conflicting opinions. We are each entitled to our views on these issues, and it seems to me, that resolving the debate in favor of either side is respectfully not the role of government. The role of government would appear to be to balance the respective rights of all those involved. The majority of us, even if we disagree on the morality or propriety of abortions, appear to agree that *Roe v. Wade* roughly struck such a balance. As such, it would not appear to be the government's role to force either a pure pro-choice or pro-life resolution to these issues. Rather, the government and the courts should continue to strike a balance on this important issue based on their limited role, a role that does not include arbitrating moral, ethical, or religious issues but allowing each of us to make our own choices.

CHAPTER 24

A FINAL NOTE..."SWITCHING IT UP"

There are few "all-or-nothings," where one side is completely right and the other side is wrong. We often, however, adopt such absolutisms through the filter of our political beliefs or points of view. These absolutisms are, as discussed above, a key component of the divisiveness of political discourse today.

Since it is current, and to demonstrate this, let's take a series of recent controversial, divisive political issues involving the 2016 election, President Trump, Joe and Hunter Biden, Hillary Clinton, and the various partisans on either side of these issues.

Let's examine these issues unfiltered by points of view or beliefs, just the facts. Where facts may be uncertain, let's consider what the conclusion would be from a hypothetical set of facts to see if we can agree once those facts become known.

As we'll see, the problem often is that when we view facts through point-of-view lenses, we come to illogical and inconsistent conclusions that can increase, and have increased, divisiveness.

One way to avoid that point-of-view filter is to "switch it up"—

that is, consider the same set of facts done by a different actor, one with whom our point of view aligns (if the original actor is contrary to our point of view) or one with whom our point of view doesn't align (if the original actor is aligned with our point of view).

Let's begin, in no particular order:

Former President Bill Clinton getting on a private plane with Attorney General Loretta Lynch weeks before the election and while an FBI investigation of his wife, then Presidential Candidate Hillary Clinton, is ongoing.

If you're a Clinton supporter, substitute Rudy Giuliani for Bill Clinton, Bill Barr for Loretta Lynch, and Donald Trump for Hillary Clinton.

Can we all agree that regardless of our point of view that this type of meeting would create an appearance of impropriety and would cause us to suspect potential improper influence of a pending federal investigation?

Candidate Donald Trump's son and others associated with his campaign agreeing to meet and then meeting with an operative of a foreign country when the stated purpose is to provide "dirt" on candidate Clinton.

Again, if you're a Donald Trump supporter, please substitute Hillary Clinton's daughter, Chelsea Clinton, for Donald Trump's son, and Candidate Trump for Candidate Clinton.

Can we all agree that even taking such a meeting is inappropriate, and can we also all agree that the appropriate response is to explicitly reject such a meeting and state that We the People of the United States do not tolerate any type of foreign interference in our elections?

Then Candidate Donald Trump encouraging (whether in jest or not) that the "Russians" hack computer servers to obtain candidate Clinton emails?

Again, if you're a Donald Trump supporter, please substitute Hillary Clinton for Donald Trump and Candidate Trump for Candidate Clinton.

Can we all agree that encouraging a foreign government to hack into the computer systems of another U.S. citizen, especially an opposing candidate, even if in jest, is inappropriate?[184]

James Comey taking copies of government documents home and putting them in a safe and sharing a copy of at least one of them with a friend, who subsequently provided the document to the media.

Again, if you need to substitute someone for James Comey to take point of view out, put in former Attorney General Jeff Sessions.

Can we all agree that as the head of the FBI, it was inappropriate for Comey to have removed such government documents and shared them outside government employees with a need to know for any reason? Rather, he should have reported the matter to the relevant inspector general or to an authorized, independent official, along with his concerns.

President Trump claiming, in direct contradiction to the express language of the Mueller Report, that the report exonerated him on obstruction of justice when it clearly did not, and Attorney General Barr not contradicting this clearly false statement.

Again, if you're a Trump supporter, please substitute President Obama for President Trump, and former Attorney General Eric Holder for Attorney General Barr.

Can we all agree that a president should not blatantly lie about a federal investigation and that an attorney general should correct such a lie?

Representative Rashida Tlaib stating on the day she was elected, referring to President Trump, "We're going to impeach the M…F…"

Again, if you are a Democrat, please substitute your favorite Republican congressional representative for Rashida Tlaib, and President Obama for President Trump. Can we all agree that making such a vulgar statement is not becoming of a congressional representative, regardless of your feelings about any president?

Can we also all agree that making such a statement is actually counter to the stated objective since it shows you've already made up your mind to take a negative action against someone even before there is a basis for taking that action?

President Trump and his spokespersons questioning the patriotism of congressionally subpoenaed witnesses who provide testimony he views as unfavorable and calling them "Never Trumpers" without any evidence in an attempt to discredit their testimony.

If you are a Trump supporter, please substitute Hillary Clinton or Bill Clinton for President Trump and "Clinton haters" for "Never Trumpers."

Can we all agree that any president or presidential candidate should not, without specific facts and basis, question the patriotism of those who disagree with him or her and should not name-call such individuals? Rather, if there are specific facts that support the proposition that facts in a witness's testimony is not true, the president or presidential candidate should come forward with facts to demonstrate that, without personally attacking opposing witnesses. Quite frankly, when such statements come from someone in high authority, it is nothing less than witness intimidation.

Using a personal attorney, without security clearance or compliance with requirements that apply to government officials, to conduct official business with foreign governments on behalf of his or her presidential client and to attempt to get foreign governments to assist the president in his reelection campaign by investigating a future or past rival.

Can we all agree that such an action, especially when designed to achieve a personal political goal, is inappropriate?

Hunter Biden, the son of then Vice President Joe Biden, taking a very highly paid position with a foreign company that is within the area of influence of his father.

Again, if you are a Democrat or Joe Biden supporter, please substitute Donald Trump Jr. and President Trump for Hunter and Joe Biden, respectively.

Although not illegal, would we all agree that such a situation would create an appearance of impropriety? Conversely, could we also agree that such an appearance of impropriety wouldn't excuse the president from asking the foreign government to announce an investigation of his opponent's family member? If anything, an investigation should be conducted by the United States, using established, nonbiased processes.

There are many other examples we could use, but I think these demonstrate the following points:

1. The same (or similar) sets of facts can generate different responses based on our political point of view, rather than the actual facts.
2. When we view facts through a point-of-view lens, we often excuse behavior that is clearly inappropriate if the actor is someone with whom we agree, and we condemn the actor if it is someone with whom we disagree, even if the facts are not worthy of that condemnation.
3. These politicians and their partisan supporters have difficulty acknowledging mistakes and taking responsibility for those mistakes, and their opponents tend to overemphasize and over condemn those mistakes while ignoring their own.

What is particularly insidious about this is not only that these things occur but, more importantly, that doing this is part of a deliberate attempt to get us, We the People, to become disillusioned about our political institutions and to not know what to believe.

Let's be very clear about how this is done:

• Repeating a lie, even a blatant lie, again and again and again with such conviction and force in an attempt to cause us to believe the lie.

- When faced with an unfavorable fact, to attack the person presenting the fact to draw attention away from the unfavorable fact.

- When the above doesn't work, attempt to make something that is bad seem less worse because it isn't something *even* worse. (This is similar to what some of our teenage children may have done to excuse rule-breaking behavior, as in, "Well, at least I'm not doing drugs.") Just because we haven't done something egregious doesn't mean that we don't have to bear the consequences (appropriate and proportional) for what we have done, or that all behavior that's less than the worst behavior should be accepted.

- Or similarly, accuse someone else of something and say what they did is just as bad or worse to excuse one's own bad actions. (Again, those of us who had or have teenage children have heard this one, too, and some of us may have used this on our parents: "Well, look at Suzie and Johnny. They did [insert their bad behavior here] and their parents didn't do anything, so I shouldn't be punished for what I did.")

As a result, more of us, We the People, are disillusioned about government and the media, and often our response is to just shrug our shoulders and accept increasingly unacceptable behavior from our leaders. Knowing this, these leaders continue to engage in increasingly bad behavior.

The most disturbing example of this, whether or not it is true, but just because it was said and by whom it was said, is President Trump's statement that "he could shoot someone in the middle of Fifth Avenue in New York City and not lose a single supporter." Put aside what you think about Donald Trump. Insert Hillary Clinton or another partisan opposite instead. Shouldn't it bother us all that our highest political leader, our president, would make such a statement? And shouldn't it bother us even more if it is true?

CONCLUSION AND CALL TO ACTION

Hopefully, you have gained a better understanding of the governmental entities (federal, state, and local; executive, legislative, and judicial) that serve us, We the People, as they relate to the issues that most affect us. We have also explored the causes of the lack of civility in public discourse and the tools and process that we can use to increase civility in that public discourse. Finally, we have explored how we can use those tools to solve many of the most controversial and important issues we face today.

The underlying thesis of this discussion is twofold: first, that We the People have the power to change the lack of civility in political discourse and to solve even the most controversial issues; second, that the vast majority of us, say 75 to 80 percent of us, have traditionally been silent on these issues although we are in agreement as to both our dissatisfaction with the current state and are in substantial agreement on many key parts of these issues.

The question is, given that power, that dissatisfaction, and that agreement, will we now act?

Since we have hopefully removed one of the biggest obstacles to acting—that is, the belief that we lack power to change a situation with which we are dissatisfied—the other remaining obstacle is the lack of concrete, actionable steps each of us can take to effect that change.

Let's identify those steps and commit to them.

- In each debate of these issues, let's focus on the policy and not the personal.
- In each debate of these issues, let's separate the facts from the spin, using the tools we already use in many other aspects of our lives to do just that, including the ones mentioned in chapter 4, in parts 2 and 3, and using "switching it up," discussed in the last chapter.
- Let's recognize the value of the rights we have in our country and hold up our end of the bargain by being citizens who are informed and who participate in getting the facts. Let us also commit to participate in the process even and especially when we feel like we are not being heard.
- Let's challenge those with whom we agree on a policy or position just as much as we challenge those with whom we disagree.
- In each debate of these issues, let's follow this process:
  - Begin with identifying a common, mutual purpose on which we can form a consensus. Ask: what is the issue we are trying to solve and what are the concerns related to that issue?
  - Gather the facts relevant to that issue, testing whether they are indeed relevant and indeed facts.
  - Consider potential solutions to some or all of the issues based on those facts and consistent with the mutual purpose.

- Let's immediately but respectfully call out anyone who deviates from having a constructive, fact-based, and non-divisive discussion of any issue.
- Let's also realize that any real change does not happen immediately but gradually. Therefore, let's commit to being patient and to persevere to achieve that change, because if we do not begin to take these actions today and to continue them each and every day from now on relentlessly, things will not only not change but will also only get worse.

Far too often, we have settled for leaders who are less than what we deserve. We have traded promises and false hopes for real solutions. We have traded manipulative spin for real facts, and based on that spin, we have dismissed facts that we know are true. We have settled for divisiveness in words or actions based on emotional appeals, especially villainization of opposing viewpoints, people, or unpopular minorities. We have settled for leaders who are poor role models for our children and ourselves, who do and say things that we know are offensive and just plain wrong, believing (falsely) that this is acceptable because they say so, as they point fingers at others to divert attention from their own unacceptable words and actions, claiming that they are the victims, even though we know that they are not. We are manipulatively spurred to action based on claims that these leaders are listening to us or working for us when it is obvious that they are really working only for themselves, their power, their financial benefit, and/or their egos.

Because we have settled, we have only encouraged more of the same, and it has caused us to solve fewer problems, not more; to become more divisive, not more united; and to become less heard, not more heard. Each time this happens, we become more disillusioned, less involved, and less empowered.

We should never have settled, and we do not need to anymore. We have the power. We have the power to end the lack of civility in our discussions of the many significant issues we face today. We have the power to solve many aspects of most of these issues. We always have.

The power of We the People.

ACKNOWLEDGMENTS

"Alone, we can do so little; together, we can do so much."

—HELEN KELLER

Anything truly meaningful is rarely based only on individual accomplishment. Anything that any one of us accomplishes is the result of people and experiences throughout our lives. Some of these are deep and long-standing, others brief but impactful.

With deep gratitude for the people and experiences that have shaped my life (so far), I would like to thank:

My family, especially my wife, Mary, who trusted and encouraged me throughout my career, even when it meant exceptional sacrifice, especially when she cared for our four children who, at the time, were all under the age of five, while I worked one-hundred-hour weeks on one of the most significant projects in my career. And, also, for supporting the initial phase of my "second career" (aka writing this book) after I retired from my "first career." Mary, without you, I could never have had the personal and professional experiences that enabled me to write this book.

My children, Ryan, Sarah, Kate, and Megan, thank you for your understanding, love, and patience with me and for teaching me what it means to be a father. I am so very proud of each of you. Sarah and Megan, special thanks for your help reviewing and editing the book in its various iterations.

My dad, my true hero, whom I lost way too soon. Although he had only an eighth-grade formal education, he taught me more than anyone else in my life. Although it's been almost a half century since you were here with me, I miss you more than can be imagined.

My mom, whom I have also lost, albeit more recently. Having lost your family at an early age, you valued our family more than anything else and taught me to do the same. Thank you for providing me with the best at-home preschool education that any child could have had.

My teachers and mentors:

My elementary school teachers, Sandra Middleton and the late Robert J. Frentzel, who each gave me the freedom and encouragement to approach learning with curiosity and creativity, even and especially when it was outside the traditional curriculum and even when I drove them crazy with that curiosity and creativity.

My high school teachers, Mrs. Emilie Roehrkasse and Mrs. Doris Wunderlich. You each saw something in me I didn't see myself. Miss Emilie, without you, I would never have discovered that I should become a lawyer and business leader or have had an amazing career doing exactly that. Mrs. Wunderlich, you taught me how to write succinctly and impactfully. Even more importantly, the emotional support you provided after my father died enabled me to overcome the many obstacles I faced as an outsider in a new school and new community.

My high school principal, Mrs. Frances Dreyer, thank you for encouraging me to pursue a legal and business career, even though standardized tests said I should be an engineer, mathematician, or scientist. Thanks also for your patient and expert guidance, which was so invaluable to me as a first-generation college student. Your wisdom and support not only ensured that I would be successful in college but enabled me to obtain the scholarships I needed to afford a college education. Congratulations on recently celebrating your 100th birthday!

My introductory political science honors professor, Dr. Harriet Imrey. I remember getting back my first test from you, with a note to come see you. I guess I should have expected that to happen, even though I did well. I wrote a detailed explanation for every false answer I gave in the true/false section of the test. (A little overkill, perhaps, but I was nervous about getting an "A" in the first class in my major.) You helped me explore politics and its intersection with economics and other disciplines as though I was taking a 300-level, not a 100-level, course. I still have the copy of John Kenneth Galbraith's *The Age of Uncertainty* that you gave me.

To my friend and executive and career coach, Jody Michael, who helped me find my "second career" and told me to write this book and to write it now. (Anyone who knows Jody knows you wouldn't dare say "no" or even "maybe" to her. I certainly wouldn't.) Jody, thanks for always challenging me to be my best self.

To Pat Banks, my friend and my other executive coach (yes, I needed more than one), who taught me the need to explain the "why" to my team, to colleagues, and even to my boss and not assume they already knew. (It may well have been the fastest lesson I ever learned: Pat threatened to tattoo the letter "Y" on my hand where it naturally forms between one's thumb and forefinger, knowing that I'm not a big fan of needles.)

The leaders who taught me leadership:

The extraordinary Ameritech executive leadership team, including Neil Cox, Barry Allen, Tom Hester, and Dick Notebaert. I was so privileged to have had the opportunity to learn from and to work for and with each of you. Thanks to each of you for giving me opportunities to utilize my business and legal skills outside the law department and especially for the opportunity to lead the teams negotiating agreements with our competitors and state regulators to implement the most significant change in telecommunications law in more than a half century. I know you took a big risk on me. I will never forget that fact and the amazing experiences you allowed me to have. Tom, I will always be grateful to you for hiring me as an antitrust lawyer, although I hadn't even taken an antitrust course in law school.

The "Scribe Tribe": You each, and as a "tribe," made publication of my first book much easier than I could ever have imagined. Special thanks to Ellie Cole, Cristina Ricci, Hal Clifford, Radha Pyari Sandhir, Libby Allen, Rachael Brandenburg, Michael Nagin, Veronica Daehn Harvey, Joyce Li, and Candace Sinclair. Veronica, Joyce, and Candace, thanks for your exceptional job copy editing and proofing the book. Michael and Rachael, thanks for designing an incredible cover that visualizes the unifying discussions we need to restore solutions and civility to U.S. politics. Libby, thanks for helping confirm the preliminary book title and then making it so much better. Hal and Radha, thank you for your editorial review of the book—your excellent comments vastly improved it. Cristina, thanks for crafting the back cover copy, combining my numerous, sometimes conflicting ideas, to ensure it captured the book's essence. And Ellie, thank you for your guidance and extraordinary patience with me during this entire process. I cannot begin to express my appreciation for your amazing responsiveness to my never-ending questions, your calming reassurances to my first-time author insecurities, and for your patient teaching (and sometimes re-teaching) me about the publishing process.

Scott Stantis, the nationally syndicated editorial cartoonist, for allowing me to use the editorial cartoon that appears at the beginning of the book, and his kind comments on my caption for the cartoon, which was a winning entry in his cartoon caption contest in the *Chicago Tribune*.

Those who serve and have served our country, especially those who made the ultimate sacrifice of their lives in doing so: Your service and sacrifice are constant reminders that our country is worth that service and sacrifice. None of us would enjoy the freedoms and blessings we have as a nation without your service and your sacrifice. We are all eternally grateful to you.

And finally, to those of you who also care deeply about our country and who are committed to increasing civics knowledge and civility in public discourse: It is you, it is us, who have the power, working together, to discover unifying solutions to solve the many pressing issues facing our nation today. Thank you for your commitment to do so. Together, we can do so much.

ABOUT THE AUTHOR

H. EDWARD (ED) WYNN has spent more than three decades helping companies, governments, and people find and implement practical solutions to complex, often divisive issues. In government, Ed worked on both "sides of the aisle" and considers himself a political independent. Ed received his bachelor's degree in political science with highest distinction from the University of Illinois, was a 1980 Truman Presidential Scholar, and received his law degree with high honors from Georgetown, where he was on the editorial board of the *Georgetown Law Journal* and taught legal research and writing. As a C-suite executive in both business and legal roles, Ed repeatedly demonstrated an ability to simplify complex issues and make them meaningful to people at all levels, both inside and outside the organizations he led. He is not afraid to tackle the most difficult and controversial issues, even if under personal attack. Ed is not a political insider and has very little, if any, name recognition with any of the political establishments. He sees that as a unique advantage, though, and hopes you will, too.

NOTES

1   See, e.g., https://www.annenbergpublicpolicycenter.org/americans-knowledge-of-the-branches-of-government-is-declining/; see also "The State of Civics Education," Center for American Progress, https://www.americanprogress.org/issues/education-k-12/reports/2018/02/21/446857/state-civics-education/.

2   See, e.g., https://ysa.org/4-reasons-young-people-dont-vote-and-what-to-do-about-it/.

3   See, e.g., Mary Soley, "If It's Controversial, Why Teach It?" *Social Education* 60, no. 1 (National Council for the Social Studies, 1996).

4   Yes, we haven't yet had a female president. However, I note that there has never been a constitutional prohibition of having a female president (even if she couldn't vote before the passage of the Nineteenth Amendment), and we will (perhaps sooner than later) have a female president.

5   See https://www.cbsnews.com/news/election-2016s-price-tag-6-8-billion/.

6   See https://www.thoughtco.com/presidential-election-campaign-fund-pecf-3367923.

7   For the approximately 10 percent of you who checked the box on your tax returns to give $3 to the Presidential Election Campaign Fund, that money is contributed to pediatric cancer research. See Gabriella Miller Kids First Research Act (H.R. 2019; 113th Congress).

8   See, e.g., https://www.cnn.com/2019/07/20/politics/obama-bundlers-like-joe-biden-pete-buttigieg/index.html. Biden lost a key bundler after his performance in the first 2020 Democratic presidential debate: https://www.politico.com/story/2019/06/28/joe-biden-fundraising-2020-1389857. But he was quick to replace that bundler so as not to lose momentum: https://www.msn.com/en-us/money/markets/joe-biden-lines-up-backing-from-paramount-ceo-after-losing-bundler-in-wake-of-debate-performance/ar-AADKfl4.

9   Super PACs proliferated as a result of the Supreme Court's decision in a case called *Citizens United*. The free speech provision of the First Amendment prohibits restrictions on individuals or entities advocating on behalf of a political viewpoint or candidate. Direct contributions of money can be restricted, notwithstanding the First Amendment, because money is not speech. Because super PACs use their funds for their own advocacy of a candidate or position, that activity cannot be prohibited.

10   https://www.politico.com/story/2019/06/29/kamala-harris-biden-debate-1390512

11   See, e.g., https://www.bloomberg.com/news/articles/2019-06-28/biden-defends-civil-rights-record-after-harris-debate-exchange and https://www.chicagotribune.com/politics/ct-pete-buttigieg-rainbow-push-20190702-62zvci5sw5hrribfmlnqpuso7a-story.html.

12   See https://www.politico.com/story/2019/08/10/harris-lands-key-iowa-endorsement-1456242.

13   Rush Limbaugh and others attempted to do this in 2008, calling their strategy Operation Chaos. See, e.g., https://www.keranews.org/post/can-voters-loyal-one-party-cause-chaos-other-party-s-primary.

14   See, e.g., https://www.pbs.org/weta/washingtonweek/blog-post/what-are-superdelegates-and-yes-republicans-have-them-too. This is not an issue in the Republican Party where superdelegates are bound to vote for the candidate who won their state's primary or caucus, which raises the question: why have them at all?

15   The District of Columbia, although it has no congressional representation, gets three electoral votes. See Twenty-Third Amendment to the Constitution.

16   In Maine and Nebraska, an electoral vote is assigned to the winner of each of the state's congressional districts (two in Maine and three in Nebraska) and the overall winner in the state is awarded the remaining two electoral votes in each state.

17   See https://www.npr.org/2016/11/02/500112248/how-to-win-the-presidency-with-27-percent-of-the-popular-vote.

18   In the 1960 presidential election, President Kennedy was elected president in an Electoral College landslide (303–219), even though he did not win the popular vote. Earlier, Woodrow Wilson (1912), Harry S Truman (1948), and Richard Nixon (1968) all won without winning the popular vote.

19   There are also states that almost always correctly pick the winner of the presidential race. These states, currently Ohio (no Republican president has ever won without carrying Ohio) and Maryland (only once—in 1948—has a Democrat won the presidency without carrying Maryland), are called litmus-test states or bellwether states. Ohio has correctly predicted the presidential outcome more than any other state: thirty-four times out of thirty-eight. Because of their track record, these states are highly influential because they help identify candidates who are leading or lagging and therefore which candidates can attract more money and influence.

20   The transcript may be found at https://www.cnn.com/2019/06/27/politics/read-rex-tillerson-house-transcript-jared-kushner/index.html.

21   Id. at 24 ff.

22   See, e.g., https://www.washingtonpost.com/politics/the-influence-industry-obama-gives-administration-jobs-to-some-big-fundraisers/2012/03/06/gIQA9y3txR_story.html and https://my.vanderbilt.edu/davidlewis/files/2011/12/The-Politics-of-Patronage-Horton-Lewis-MW.pdf.

23   See, e.g., https://www.nbcchicago.com/blogs/ward-room/blagojevich-trial-politicians-reaction-100953089.html ; see also https://townhall.com/tipsheet/guybenson/2018/06/05/mr-president-corrupt-democrat-rod-blagojevich-does-not-deserve-a-pardon-n2487231.

24   Throughout our entire history, Congress has overturned presidential vetoes very rarely. Of 2,579 vetoes, only 111 were overturned, or about 4 percent of the time. https://history.house.gov/Institution/Presidential-Vetoes/Presidential-Vetoes/.

25   Johnson does have the distinction of having the most overridden vetoes at fifteen; even though he had more than 50 percent of his vetoes overridden, another president, Pierce, has the record for the greatest percentage of overridden vetoes at 56 percent.

26   Presidents Grant and Franklin Roosevelt had supermajorities in both houses during some portion of their presidencies. Their vetoes that were overturned occurred only in those years in which they did not have a supermajority.

27   See https://www.history.com/topics/us-government/executive-order, and see https://www.nbcnews.com/politics/white-house/here-s-full-list-donald-trump-s-executive-orders-n720796 for a list of the executive orders under President Trump.

28   See https://www.aol.com/article/news/2017/01/28/president-trump-breaks-obamas-record-of-most-executive-actions/21701658/.

29   E.g., President Franklin Roosevelt used an executive order for the forced internment of more than 100,000 Japanese Americans, among other things.

30   This has more recently been done in so-called signing statements, issued at the time the president signs legislation, detailing what portions of that legislation the executive branch will not enforce. Up until the Reagan administration, a combined total of seventy-five signing statements were issued; subsequent presidents have, in total, issued more than 250 signing statements.

31   In addition to Congress, under the Independent Counsel Act, a designated official in the Justice Department, part of the executive branch, can conduct investigations of the president and the executive branch. This is, by the way, how Rod Rosenstein (an assistant attorney general) derived his power to institute and oversee the Russia Election Interference Investigation, conducted by Special Counsel Robert Mueller.

32 Notably, more is not always better here. When one party has too sizable a party majority in both houses, other divisions can develop within the party that can be at odds with the party's policy objectives. An analysis of this phenomenon in Illinois was the subject of the author's undergraduate senior honors thesis.

33 See, e.g., https://qz.com/1657742/
ideological-alliances-and-divides-on-the-us-supreme-court-charted/.

34 See, e.g., https://fivethirtyeight.com/features/is-chief-justice-roberts-a-secret-liberal/.

35 The president is not immune from a civil action during his or her term, although the trial in such a civil action cannot occur until after the president leaves office.

36 Whether or not the Department of Justice precedent would be applied to a state, as opposed to a federal, criminal case is unclear.

37 Why do we call this gerrymandering? In 1812, Massachusetts Governor Elbridge Gerry led an effort to define new legislative districts to give disproportionate representation to his party. The outline of one of those districts resembled a salamander, as depicted in a satirical cartoon in the *Boston Gazette*.

38 In the seven states that have only one congressional district, this is not an issue since the state boundary serves as the congressional district boundary. Only four states (Arizona, California, Colorado, and Michigan) have adopted an independent method to determine the boundaries. In the rest, it's up to the state legislature or processes that involve state legislators or political appointees. See https://www.brennancenter.org/our-work/research-reports/who-draws-maps-legislative-and-congressional-redistricting. Challenges to this process are rarely successful.

39 See, e.g., https://www.chicagotribune.com/politics/ct-illinois-supreme-court-independent-map-ruling-met-0826-20160825-story.html.

40 See, e.g., https://www.washingtonpost.com/news/wonk/wp/2016/06/09/how-a-widespread-practice-to-politically-empower-african-americans-might-actually-harm-them/.

41 See https://www.brennancenter.org/our-work/analysis-opinion/
does-anti-gerrymandering-campaign-threaten-minority-voting-rights.

42 See, e.g., http://www.msnbc.com/hardball/how-much-does-it-cost-win-seat-congre.

43 See, e.g., https://www.thoughtco.com/
bundling-political-contributions-legal-and-illegal-3367621.

44 Although it is absolutely true that some incumbents have lost elections, those instances are rare or are aligned with macro political party changes, such as in the 2018 congressional elections.

45 See https://www.congress.gov/members?q=%7B"party"%3A"Independent"%7D.

46 Although the vice president is technically the president of the Senate, he or she is not the leader of the Senate.

47 As a part of current Speaker Pelosi's deal to regain the Speaker position, she agreed to a four-term limit for party leaders. However, that "deal" can easily be modified or eliminated at a later time.

48 See https://www.opensecrets.org/overview/cand2cand.php; see also https://www.minnpost.com/eric-black-ink/2017/04/congressional-dues-help-garner-good-committee-assignments/.

49 See, e.g., https://www.politico.com/story/2019/01/15/pelosi-rice-judiciary-committee-1102772. There are Republican Party examples, too. This is just the most recent example.

50 See, e.g., https://www.opensecrets.org/elections/.

51 See https://www.cagw.org/reporting/pig-book#summary.

52 See https://www.cbsnews.com/news/60-minutes-are-members-of-congress-becoming-telemarketers/.

53 As discussed further below, this is why we advocate for greater and more simplified, publicly available information about these activities.

54 See, e.g., https://www.termlimits.com/congress-fundraising-priority/.

55 See https://www.politifact.com/truth-o-meter/article/2016/mar/17/context-biden-rule-supreme-court-nominations/.

56 See https://www.vox.com/2018/6/29/17511088/scotus-2016-election-poll-trump-republicans-kennedy-retire.

57 See, e.g., https://www.cnn.com/2018/09/17/politics/dianne-feinstein-brett-kavanaugh-allegations/index.html.

58 See https://history.house.gov/Institution/Origins-Development/Investigations-Oversight/.

59 See, e.g., https://www.acc.com/sites/default/files/program-materials/upload/2019-03-26 Akin Gump-Congressional Investigations-PPTX.pdf.

60 See, e.g., https://www.politico.com/story/2017/08/17/trump-russia-investigation-congress-fundraising-241491.

61 See, e.g., https://www.washingtonpost.com/politics/2019/07/24/during-muellers-testimony-some-members-congress-will-grandstand-heres-logic-behind-which-ones-will/.

62 There are other limited jurisdiction federal courts—for example, the U.S. Court for International Trade, the U.S. Federal Claims Court. Because of their limited jurisdiction, they are not discussed here.

63 Only once has a Supreme Court justice, Samuel Chase, been impeached by the House; however, he was acquitted by the Senate. To date, only fourteen federal court judges have been impeached; eight were convicted, three were acquitted, and three resigned.

64 Since the Clinton administration, ten presidential judicial nominees have been rated as Not Qualified by the American Bar Association (ABA). Three Clinton nominees were so rated; all were confirmed. One George W. Bush nominee was so rated and was confirmed. Six Trump nominees were so rated: both circuit court nominees were confirmed, two of the four district court nominees were confirmed, one withdrew, and one remains pending. A recent analysis of ABA ratings by the *Political Research Quarterly* found some pro-Democratic nominee bias in the ratings, largely on the issue of whether a nominee had previous political experience. See Smelcer et al., "Bias and the Bar: Evaluating the ABA Ratings of Federal Judiciary Nominees," *Political Research Quarterly*, December 2011.

65 See https://www.uscourts.gov/sites/default/files/apptsbypres.pdf for list of appointments by president.

66 Notably, none of this process, other than the fact that the president nominates federal judges and the Senate confirms them, is constitutionally required. This process has developed on its own, and therefore, we have the power to change it.

67 That Democrats were surprised by the use of this "rule" during the Garland Supreme Court nomination is at best, disingenuous. Like Republicans, they have used the same "rule" for Republican presidential nominees. See, e.g., Rutkus and Scott, "Nomination and Confirmation of Lower Federal Court Judges in Presidential Election Years," *Congressional Research Service*, August 13, 2008.

68 See https://fas.org/sgp/crs/misc/R45622.pdf.

69 President Trump has further identified members of the federal judiciary, not only by the political party of the president that appointed them but identifying them with the specific president who appointed them—for example, "Obama" judges.

70 The only partial exception to this is the state of Louisiana, whose state legal system is, for some matters, code based.

71 A notable example is the failed nomination of Robert Bork. See, e.g., https://www.theatlantic.com/politics/archive/2012/12/the-sad-legacy-of-robert-bork/266456/. It even led to a new political verb, "borked," which means "to obstruct (someone, especially a candidate for public office) through systematic defamation or vilification."

72 Notably, all but two of the remaining fifteen states allow an individual to serve in the legislature for at least sixteen years.

73 That's right: to us! We'll return to this very important point later.

74 See, e.g., https://oag.ca.gov/sites/all/files/agweb/pdfs/sb657/resource-guide.pdf.

75 See, e.g., https://www.harryanddavid.com/h/view/CA-SB-657-Disclosure?ref=bing_search_nontm&msclkid=300d1535fa831b74948048de38c5c685&utm_source=bing&utm_medium=cpc&utm_campaign=b_nontm_dsa_desktop_categories&utm_term=harryanddavid&utm_content=All Webpages.

76 See, e.g., https://hbr.org/2018/07/
    what-you-need-to-know-about-californias-new-data-privacy-law.

77 See id.; see also https://www.dickinson-wright.com/news-alerts/
    californias-data-privacy-law and https://thehill.com/opinion/
    technology/472834-should-congress-be-concerned-about-californias-data-privacy-law.

78 See, e.g., https://releases.jhu.edu/2018/12/11/
    jhu-survey-americans-dont-know-much-about-state-government/.

79 See id.

80 Of course, there are many exceptions to this rule, including in my current home state, Illinois,
    involving former governors Blagojevich and Ryan. Each of these, however, became a "national
    interest" story.

81 See, e.g., https://publicintegrity.org/federal-politics/state-politics/state-integrity-investigation/
    how-does-your-state-rank-for-integrity/. Based on this study and ranking on the criteria of
    public access to information, three states received a grade of C–; one each received grades of
    D+, D, and D–, respectively; and the remaining forty-four states each earned an F.

82 See, e.g., https://www.logikcull.com/blog/state-open-records-heat-map.

83 See, e.g., http://www.abajournal.com/magazine/article/officials_public_records_personal_
    email; https://www.kansascity.com/news/politics-government/article236562098.html. Notably,
    some local governments provide more access to public proceedings than state governments.
    For example, many local governments post live or recorded meeting videos on public
    access channels.

84 See https://www.chicagotribune.com/politics/ct-luis-arroyo-replacement-challenge-20191130-
    vyvtprnybbae3eb56apq5f2tcu-story.html.

85 Unlike the U.S., fourteen state governors do not have term limits, and only seven have a lifetime
    two-term limit similar to that of the U.S. presidency. Unlike the U.S. executive branch, most
    states (forty-four) elect one or more executive offices, such as secretary of state or attorney general.
    (As you'll recall, the president appoints these individuals—they are not elected.) These elected
    executive officials can be, are, and have been from a different political party than the governor
    and rarely have term limits. In the federal government, since the officials are appointed by the
    president and serve "at the pleasure of the president," their term is limited by the president's.

86 See, e.g., https://www.chicagotribune.com/investigations/ct-madigan-13th-ward-quinn-
    election-20191010-6p6bexkfr5htnpbontth2dixeq-story.html.

87 https://harvardpolitics.com/united-states/
    stealing-in-the-shadows-state-level-political-corruption/

88 My home state of Illinois holds the record of most such governors: four. See
    also https://www.npr.org/sections/itsallpolitics/2014/09/04/345867847/
    from-statehouse-to-big-house-a-guide-to-governors-gone-bad.

89 See https://publicintegrity.org/federal-politics/state-politics/state-integrity-investigation/only-three-states-score-higher-than-d-in-state-integrity-investigation-11-flunk/. No state scored above a C–, and eleven states had grades of F. See also https://harvardpolitics.com/united-states/stealing-in-the-shadows-state-level-political-corruption/.

90 See, e.g., https://www.latimes.com/politics/la-pol-ca-california-government-nepotism-persists-20190501-story.html and https://www.propublica.org/article/cook-county-assessors-old-school-politics-come-with-a-price-for-taxpayers.

91 Ten have outright bans on outside employment; six others provide for limited exceptions; twenty-three permit outside employment without any restrictions; the rest permit it with minimal restrictions.

92 See, e.g., https://www.illinoispolicy.org/investigation-madigan-firm-the-biggest-player-in-commercial-property-tax-appeals/.

93 https://ballotpedia.org/Judicial_selection_in_the_states. Fifteen states use a "merit-based" system, which relies on nominations from a nonpartisan judicial nominating body; twenty-two states elect judges (in eight of these states, the judges run with a political party affiliation); in four states, judges are appointed (in two of these, by the governor; in the other two, by the legislature); and the remaining nine states use a mixed system. In ten states (and the District of Columbia), some type of legislative confirmation is required for some, most, or all courts.

94 For example, in my current home state of Illinois, the Democratic-majority Supreme Court has uniformly sided with the Illinois Speaker of the House in preventing a voter referendum on term limits. See, e.g., https://www.governing.com/news/headlines/term-limit-referendum-gets-another-setback-in-illinois.html.

95 For example, in many, if not most or all, of these elections, judicial candidates receive political contributions. Little information is readily available to ascertain influence based on those political contributions. Yet, obtaining contributions is required as part of the election process for a candidate to be elected, unless, of course, the candidate is wealthy enough to self-finance his or her campaign, which raises other issues.

96 Please see the following references that generally describe this issue and support the points made in this section: https://www.nasra.org/files/Issue%20Briefs/NASRACostsBrief.pdf, https://www.urban.org/policy-centers/cross-center-initiatives/state-and-local-finance-initiative/projects/state-and-local-backgrounders/state-and-local-government-pensions, https://www.investors.com/politics/commentary/state-pensions-underfunded/, and https://www.forbes.com/sites/johnmauldin/2019/05/20/the-coming-pension-crisis-is-so-big-that-its-a-problem-for-everyone/#117f6f4437fc; see also https://www.illinoispolicy.org/reports/pensions-101-understanding-illinois-massive-government-worker-pension-crisis/.

97 See, e.g., https://www.illinoispolicy.org/the-top-illinois-pensioners-of-2015/.

98 See, e.g., https://www.governing.com/gov-institute/voices/col-teacher-pensions-raises-nearing-retirement.html.

99 See, e.g., https://www.illinoispolicy.org/reports/
unpaid-sick-leave-spikes-illinois-teachers-pension-benefits/.

100 See, e.g., https://www.chicagotribune.com/news/ct-met-pensions-double-dip-20111012-story.
html.

101 See, generally, https://fee.org/articles/
the-5-states-with-the-most-underfunded-public-employee-pensions/.

102 See, e.g., https://www.heritage.org/budget-and-spending/commentary/
how-big-your-states-share-6-trillion-unfunded-pension-liabilities.

103 See, e.g., https://www.governing.com/finance101/gov-pension-protections-state-by-state.html.

104 See https://mitgovlab.org/updates/mapping-local-government-transparency-in-the-us/.

105 See, e.g., https://www.northjersey.com/story/news/politics/elections/2019/11/05/election-2019-
nj-few-local-candidates-challengers-limit-voters-choices/4156287002/; see, generally, https://
pdfs.semanticscholar.org/1dd7/06ddab992003bba54725cdc4efbf0df1495a.pdf.

106 See, e.g., https://www.governing.com/news/state/mct-report-45-state-officials-
linked-to-fracking-industry.html; see, generally, https://ethics.harvard.edu/blog/
measuring-illegal-and-legal-corruption-american-states-some-results-safra and https://www.
justice.gov/usao-mdpa/public-corruption-prosecutions.

107 One of the worst recent examples involved Bell, California. See http://www.wpsanet.org/
papers/docs/reilly2017.pdf.

108 See, e.g., https://www.cbsnews.com/news/
police-man-with-assault-rifle-dc-comet-pizza-victim-of-fake-sex-trafficking-story/.

109 The bias is virtually always clear from what the host says (tone or content), but if there's any
doubt, turn the volume off and watch the hosts' (and experts') facial and body expressions,
which are equally damning as to their lack of objectivity. (By the way, try this when listening
to a presidential debate, as I often do. Even if it's not as dramatic as Nixon's profuse sweating
during the debate with Kennedy, the candidates' facial and body language often says more than
their words!)

110 Interestingly, this point of view has been on both sides of the political spectrum. In the 1960s,
the liberal point of view discredited facts because they came from the "establishment." Today,
the conservative point of view discredits facts because they come from the political elite, also
known as the "swamp" or the "deep state." As interesting are the pejorative labels used in each
of these examples: "establishment," "elite," etc. Turnabout may be fair play, but not when it
affects us, We the People, and our democracy.

111 See https://www.journalism.org/2014/10/21/political-polarization-media-habits/.

112 Malcolm Gladwell's most recent book, *Talking to Strangers*, makes this important point convincingly by providing extensive data and real-life examples of how we misread strangers by attributing thoughts and actions to them based solely on their demeanor.

113 See, e.g., https://www.bbc.com/future/article/20161026-how-liars-create-the-illusion-of-truth and https://www.wired.com/2017/02/dont-believe-lies-just-people-repeat/.

114 See https://www.nationalreview.com/magazine/2016/02/15/big-liar/. ("In *Mein Kampf*, Adolf Hitler discussed the use of a lie so 'colossal' that no one would believe that someone 'could have the impudence to distort the truth so infamously.'")

115 See https://money.cnn.com/2016/11/02/media/fake-news-stories/index.html for examples.

116 See, e.g., https://www.latimes.com/local/california/la-me-berkeley-protest-shapiro-20170914-htmlstory.html.

117 To be fair, one part of the abortion debate, perhaps a significant portion of the debate, involves whether an abortion constitutes a "crime"—that is, murder. That debate, stripped of religious belief considerations, is an appropriate debate if conducted civilly and based on scientific facts.

118 For example, one way to address a bona fide religious belief regarding vaccinations is to align the right to assert such a religious belief with a corresponding responsibility. That is, you have the right not to have your child vaccinated based on such a religious belief, but you must take the responsibility that derives from that decision: your children may not participate in activities that put them in contact with other children or adults that may cause those children or adults to contract a potentially deadly disease.

119 See, e.g., https://www.journalism.org/2014/10/21/political-polarization-media-habits/.

120 Unfortunately, this is neither the only nor the most egregious example. A group of extremists protested at the funeral of Fred Rogers, Mr. Rogers of *Mr. Rogers' Neighborhood*, based on their disagreement with him over certain political issues, namely his support of gay rights. See https://www.newyorker.com/news/daily-comment/the-two-freds-when-phelps-protested-mr-rogerss-memorial. We can learn much from Fred Rogers about civility, inclusion, and problem solving. One of my favorite Mr. Rogers quotes is, "Those that make you feel less than who you are are the greatest evil."

121 See, e.g., https://www.chicagotribune.com/columns/dahleen-glanton/ct-dahleen-glanton-ellen-bush-donald-trump-forgiveness-20191014-uvyztkq7ondezcqavc2vnev54u-story.html, https://www.vox.com/culture/2019/10/9/20906371/ellen-degeneres-george-w-bush-controversy, and https://theintercept.com/2019/10/09/ellen-degeneres-george-bush/.

122 See, e.g., https://www.uscis.gov/citizenship/learners/citizenship-rights-and-responsibilities.

123 A recent example is illustrative: the whistleblower who raised issues about President Trump's withholding aid to Ukraine based on receiving a political "favor" raised those concerns in strict compliance with whistleblower laws and regulations. For that reason, he or she should be protected, and if his or her reporting is found to be consistent with other available facts, it should be deemed credible. On the other hand, a speaker who anonymously writes (for profit) a book such as *The Warning* should have substantially less credibility, both because he or she is profiting from his or her actions and because he or she failed to follow the applicable laws and regulations for reporting the matters of which he or she complains.

124 See https://www.vanityfair.com/magazine/1998/05/williams199805.

125 See, e.g., https://www.businessinsider.com/
immigrants-commit-less-crime-than-native-born-americans-trump-speech-2017-3.

126 See https://www.npr.org/2019/01/10/683662691/
where-does-illegal-immigration-mostly-occur-heres-what-the-data-tell-us.

127 See, e.g., https://www.cnn.com/politics/live-news/immigration-border-children-separation/
h_5652f6b137eaba6711e304f376476c94 and https://www.theatlantic.com/ideas/archive/2018/06/
child-separation/563252/.

128 See, e.g., https://www.psychologytoday.com/us/blog/
happiness-and-the-pursuit-leadership/201909/human-beings-are-not-insects-vermin-parasites-or.

129 Professor Greg Stanton has identified this slippery slope in his work, *The Ten Stages of Genocide*. The ten stages are (1) Classification, (2) Symbolization, (3) Discrimination, (4) Dehumanization, (5) Organization, (6) Polarization, (7) Preparation, (8) Persecution, (9) Extermination, and (10) Denial.

130 See https://scholar.harvard.edu/files/hckelman/files/Violence_1973.pdf.

131 See https://thehill.com/homenews/media/381205-ny-magazine-cover-depicts-trump-as-a-pig.

132 Personally, I think every political office holder should read (or even better, receive training in) *Crucial Conversations*. To be clear, I have no financial interest in the publisher or authors of *Crucial Conversations*, nor have I ever met with or spoken to them.

133 Glenn Beck's 9/12 Project is perhaps the most prominent example of such a manipulation of the tragedy and the national unity that resulted after 9/11.

134 At this point, I want to note and be very clear with words. Words matter. I deliberately used the word "characterize" us rather than words or phrases that create value judgments, from the potentially benign "distinguish" or directly contain a value judgment "make us great as a nation." To be clear, the latter phrase is not a value judgment on political slogans. It is used only to ensure that for purposes of determining common principles (as opposed to political slogans), we are careful not to place value judgments.

135 The preamble to the Constitution also contains a reference to "Liberty," which is contained in more specificity in the Declaration of Independence.

136 The author was the 1980 Truman Presidential Scholar from Illinois.

137 President Truman did not have a middle name, just an initial, which is why there is no period after the "S."

138 Ms. Cupp coined this phrase with specific reference to President Trump. But let's be honest with ourselves, he's not the only one who does this.

139 See, e.g., Caitlin Flanagan, "Bill Clinton: A Reckoning," *The Atlantic*, November 13, 2017, https://www.theatlantic.com/entertainment/archive/2017/11/reckoning-with-bill-clintons-sex-crimes/545729/.

140 See, e.g., https://www.cnn.com/2017/07/31/opinions/obama-romney-russia-opinion-drucker/index.html.

141 See, e.g., https://www.cbsnews.com/news/hillary-clinton-what-happened-sunday-morning-jane-pauley/.

142 See, e.g., https://thehill.com/homenews/administration/422457-trump-reverses-says-dems-to-blame-for-shutdown.

143 See, e.g., https://www.newsweek.com/trump-threatens-sue-democrats-shifty-adam-schiff-fraud-over-impeachment-1467909 (copies of actual President Trump tweets included).

144 This appears to be a reference to *The New York Times*.

145 That Trump should have personally, quickly, and strongly condemned such violence is particularly important given his prior statements encouraging physical violence against opponents. See, e.g., https://abcnews.go.com/Politics/back-trump-comments-perceived-encouraging-violence/story?id=48415766.

146 This is the thesis of Christopher Hood's book, *The Blame Game: Spin, Bureaucracy and Self-Preservation in Government*.

147 See Alice M. Rivlin, "Congress: Take a Timeout from Playing the Political Blame Game," February 12, 2018.

148 See https://www.cnn.com/2019/09/23/politics/america-in-one-room-political-discussions/index.html.

149 American Center for Political Leadership, "U.S. Voter Sentiment on First View Post-Election Research" at slide 24 (2019).

150 Id. at slide 25.

151 Id. at slide 31.

152 Id. at slide 30.

153 See Pew Research Center, "Public Highly Critical of State of Political Discourse in the U.S.," June 19, 2019.

154 See, e.g., https://www.fastcompany.com/3046246/how-facebook-just-became-the-worlds-largest-publisher.

155 See, e.g., https://www.nytimes.com/2019/09/26/technology/government-disinformation-cyber-troops.html.

156 Only a handful of libel cases against publishers are not dismissed on this ground.

157 See https://www.facebook.com/safety/groups/law/guidelines.

158 See https://www.city-journal.org/html/platform-or-publisher-15888.html.

159 The First Amendment's prohibition on censoring of information only applies to governmental actors, not private entities. Other laws provide some censorship protection.

160 To be sure, some parts of Facebook's offerings—for example, private individual pages used to share family photos—may not be subject to rules that apply to media publishers. However, many other parts of Facebook's offerings, including those that provide news or allow public comments, are clearly an electronic version of traditional media publishing. Without doubt, content that Facebook itself generates as a result of user views and its data and algorithms—see, for example, https://apnews.com/f97c24dab4f34bd0b48b36f2988952a4—makes it a publisher.

161 And if someone does want to TL; DR, then they should give up their right to express views on matters they chose not to inform themselves. When people complain about elected officials, I ask them, "Did you vote?" If the answer is no, my response is, "Then don't complain." Similarly, if you opine about a topic that you've TL; DR'd, then my response is similar: don't comment. (This goes for media professionals who, I note, opined about the Mueller Report and other documents before they read them. I think our new acronym should be DR?; DC! [Didn't read? Don't comment!].)

162 https://www.cnn.com/videos/politics/2019/11/06/pennsylvania-voter-panel-swing-part-1-camerota-newday-vpx.cnn

163 See https://www.nbcnews.com/politics/meet-the-press/blog/meet-press-blog-latest-news-analysis-data-driving-political-discussion-n988541/ncrd1076316 - blogHeader.

164 There are many variations to these potential solutions as well as many others. And for sure, they would require some type of multicountry cooperation. The purpose of identifying them is to demonstrate that there are solutions to address the economic competitiveness issue in a way that is not punitive but that appropriately recognizes the real costs of pollution and assigns them to the cost causers, as well as providing consumers information they need to select products that support global pollution reduction.

165 Tariffs are already applied to address issues of unfair competition; product surcharges have been applied to reflect costs of pollution including a "gas guzzler tax" and surcharges for disposition of automobile wastes; and the California Transparency in Supply Chains Act is an example of requiring product disclosures related to policy issues, as are other laws that require labeling the source of imported products.

166 In the interest of appropriate disclosure, the author was raised Southern Baptist, married in the Roman Catholic Church, is a converted Catholic, and has been and is in a monogamous "marriage" for more than thirty years. I believe that religious beliefs must be respected, but they should not be imposed on others. I also believe in separation of church and state and equal rights under the law.

167 Yes, I read all of it.

168 Perhaps, though, we should have expected that there would be no serious examination of Russian interference in the election since, during the 2016 presidential campaign, then candidate Trump publicly urged the Russians to interfere in the election by hacking the computer servers of the opposing political party organization.

169 That choice is the overriding issue cannot be understated both on this issue and many other significant political issues. Our heritage is based on We the People having choice, and generally, constraints on that choice are viewed very negatively, whereas maximizing or preserving choice is viewed positively.

170 Despite the fact that few of us would choose not to have health insurance, the feature of Obamacare that required everyone to have health insurance or pay a tax was a key part of the political and legal attempt to overturn Obamacare.

171 https://assets.aarp.org/rgcenter/health/fs149_medicare.pdf

172 https://www.medicaresupplement.com/articles/medigap-users-satisfaction/

173 https://www.ncbi.nlm.nih.gov/pmc/articles/PMC4193523/

174 https://www.kff.org/health-costs/press-release/
poll-acas-pre-existing-condition-protections-remain-popular-with-public/

175 A very divided U.S. Supreme Court did consider this language in *D.C. v. Heller* (2008). (The majority opinion and dissents can be found at https://www.law.cornell.edu/supct/html/07-290. ZS.html.)

176 Let me go out on a limb here and say that I suspect that the data will show exactly zero use of any weapon for militia purposes, and that even if militia purposes is distorted to include use against a gun violence perpetrator, it will be an extremely negligible percentage of such use. I make this point not for purposes of aligning with either extreme on this issue but to demonstrate that if one side (or the other) wants to base its position on the Second Amendment, it cannot do so selectively.

177 See, e.g., https://www.pewresearch.org/fact-tank/2019/10/16/share-of-americans-who-favor-stricter-gun-laws-has-increased-since-2017/ and https://www.pewresearch.org/fact-tank/2019/10/22/facts-about-guns-in-united-states/

178 505 U.S. 833 (1992)

179 See https://prolifeaction.org/fact/ and https://prolifeaction.org/fact/rapeincest/.

180 https://www.prochoiceamerica.org/issue/abortion-access/

181 See https://prolifeaction.org/fact_type/where-we-stand/.

182 https://www.prochoiceamerica.org/report/respond-to-tough-questions/

183 See https://news.gallup.com/poll/1576/abortion.aspx.

184 We'll put aside for now whether such encouragement is illegal. Again, with any of these examples, the issue at hand isn't whether they're legal or not—that's for the appropriate judicial entities to decide. The issue is to examine how We the People would expect our nation's leaders, government officials, and candidates for public office to conduct themselves.